High Praise for *Score College Schola~*

"As a coach who has helped develop at collegiate student-athletes in seven sport invaluable resource for any athlete looking  ollege."

Mark Anderson
26-time Marin Swim League Championship Coach,
Sleepy Hollow Swim Team

"Laura's step-by-step playbook provides everything that prospective student-athletes need, whether they are highly sought-after by collegiate coaches or trying to get noticed."

Ken Demont
USA Swimming Coach, North Bay Aquatics

"Laura Dickinson is an extraordinary student and even more extraordinary in her ability to lay out a plan and follow it. Her guide is a canon for high school athletes seeking to find the best and most challenging mix of studies and athletics in college or university."

G. Robert Hamrdla
Admissions Reader and Former Assistant to the President
and Professor, Stanford University

"Having watched Laura navigate and implement her recruiting process, I can tell you that she knows all the subtleties about how to find the right fit in a school and program."

Don Swartz
Hall of Fame Coach,
American Swim Coaches Association

SCORE COLLEGE SCHOLARSHIPS

The Student-Athlete's Playbook to Recruiting Success

LAURA DICKINSON
WITH ROBERT A. DICKINSON

Made for Success
PUBLISHING

Made for Success Publishing
P.O. Box 1775
Issaquah, WA 98027

If you are seeking to purchase this book in quantity for sales promotion or corporate use, please contact Made for Success at 425-657-0300 or email Sales@MadeforSuccess.net. Your local bookstore can also help you with discounted bulk purchase options.

ISBN: 978-1-64146-282-2 (Physical Book)
ISBN: 978-1-64146-283-9 (eBook)
ISBN: 978-1-64146-342-3 (Audiobook)

Library of Congress Cataloging-in-Publication data

Dickinson, Laura and Dickinson, Bob
Score College Scholarships: The Student-Athlete's Playbook to Recruiting Success
pages. Cm
1. STUDY AIDS / Financial Aid
2. EDUCATION / Higher
3. SPORTS & RECREATION / Coaching / General

Printed in the United States of America

CONTENTS

SECTION IV
TAKING CAMPUS VISITS | 155

SECTION V
GETTING PAID TO PLAY | 227

SECTION VI
MAKING DECISIONS | 253

SECTION VII
DEBUNKING THE TOP 5 MYTHS ABOUT COLLEGIATE
ATHLETIC RECRUITING | 275

PREFACE

Growing up, I won 38 team and individual championships in 27 seasons among five sports, including swimming, water polo, basketball, volleyball, and tennis. At age 10, I started swimming competitively in a recreational league. As my love of swimming flourished, I thoughtfully and meticulously dropped each of the other sports. On the way to my first high school swimming league championships as a freshman, I suffered whiplash when a sport-utility vehicle rear-ended the sedan in which I was riding.

Wanting to swim in college, I endured months of rehabilitation and rededicated myself to the sport I love. For the required Common Application essay I wrote for college admissions, I answered the question: "The lessons we take from failure can be fundamental to later success. Recount an incident or time when you experienced failure. How did it affect you, and what did you learn from the experience?" This reflects my roller-coaster to recovery:

Lessons for Life from Swimming

Sunlight glistens off lapping waves of the pool at the Santa Clara International Swim Center. Legs pumping and arms rotating, like a push mower churning across a level lawn, I rush to the wall to complete my freestyle leg of the St. Ignatius College Prep (SI) women's medley relay. A qualifying time places our team into the finals of the California Central Coast Section (CCS) Swimming Championships.

Racing for home, excruciating pain and shock waves reverberate through my body. As I touch the wall, flashbacks of the sound a sport-utility vehicle makes rear-ending our sedan a week earlier revisit my mind. Motionless well after all other competitors exit the pool, I cling lifelessly to the edge of my lane. Several teammates and timers help me from the chilly waters.

"We qualified for CCS finals!" one teammate exclaims. Unable to move, I cannot reciprocate her elation. The whiplash endured from the automobile accident settles in. I cannot move my right arm and shoulder, and eventually can lift my left arm only halfway. Not being able to anchor my team in the finals the next day and having to scratch my individual events, especially as a high school freshman, make me feel like I am failing my teammates. The satisfaction of putting my teammates above myself for that relay, however, fuels my resilience when facing months of rehabilitation.

That weekend, my club-swimming coach and I sit poolside, talk about the experience, and set goals. I learn to close my eyes, visualize the rehabilitation race, take a deep breath, and dive into the adversity.

My coach accommodates subsequent workouts, working with me at first in the diving pool away from other swimmers. He then dedicates a lane for me and helps me to see how I will be stronger after my rehabilitation. I learn that while swimming results are based on touchpads and stopwatches, quality time remains the best contributor to success.

When I fail to reach short-term goals on multiple occasions during sophomore year, I sit up in bed thinking about how I do not like training for hours every week only to swim poorly at big meets. Three options enter my mind: quit swimming, train as I have previously, or train as I never have before. Quitting is not an option and going through the motions at practice will not help me reach my potential; I want more.

For training blocks during junior year, I swim like a woman possessed. I enjoy getting out after practice, driving home, and not being able to do much because I feel so exhausted. I train 20 hours per week for 49 weeks and participate in 28 meets comprising 66 calendar days. Spring semester of my junior year, I miss 41 classes to attend invitational meets around the country. This commitment dramatically decreases the amount of time I have to study, but I believe I achieve an outstanding level of performance in the classroom and in the pool.

At an invitational meet nearly two years after the accident, I qualify for the Junior National Championships in Orlando by dropping time in four consecutive races. During the spring high school season, I anchor the SI women's medley relay team, comprised of the same team members as my freshman year, to win the CCS consolation final in come-from-behind fashion. I learn that when your circumstances flip upside down, it is possible to persevere with clear goggles and a great push from a solid wall.

Sacrificing for my team demonstrated selflessness and leadership, enduring an injury taught me how to overcome adversity, and rehabilitating fully showed me what personal sacrifice can achieve. Sometimes it is not what you accomplish that matters, but what you overcome.

As a high school Academic All-American, I competed in the NCSA Junior National Championships, USA Swimming Futures Championships, and California State High School Championships, and won three Pacific Swimming and thirteen league championships. I served as a two-time varsity team captain, earned a Coaches' Award, and garnered four letters in swimming at St. Ignatius College Prep in San Francisco. Based on a commitment in the classroom, I am a California Interscholastic Federation/Central Coast Section Scholastic Champion and four-time Scholar-Athlete Award winner. Having directed activities for underprivileged youths in my community, I am also a California Scholarship Federation Life Member and Marin County Youth Volunteer of the Year.

To honor the hard work I demonstrated to overcome adversity and become an accomplished swimmer, I conducted an intentional collegiate athletic recruiting process. During my recruiting odyssey, I ended up contacting or being contacted by 52 college coaches, including nine Division I, five Division II and 38 Division III programs. I communicated with 16 coaches at least quarterly over two years, visited 22 different campuses, submitted pre-read materials to 11 programs, and made two unofficial visits and four official visits to campuses. After applying Early Decision, I gained admission to a highly-regarded liberal arts college with a nationally-ranked and conference championship swim team. I earned six scholarships to help pay for college. Now I am an NCAA collegiate athlete in swimming.

One of the reasons I documented my recruiting experience throughout high school is to help teammates, friends, and prospective student-athletes around the country achieve their dream of competing in a collegiate sport. Throughout these pages, I share personal and sometimes poignant moments about my recruiting journey, from participating in high school and club sports to receiving recruiting offers and getting accepted to college. Prospective coaches, teammates, and fellow recruits shared information that taught me invaluable lessons about the collegiate athletic recruiting process. While the circumstances and excerpts from communications are real, I have redacted names and the colleges or universities they represent to protect their privacy. Any resemblance to a particular coach or athlete is coincidental. While my primary sport involves competitive swimming, the lessons learned from my recruiting process shared in this book may be applied by a prospective student-athlete pursuing any sport.

My mission is to help prospective student-athletes successfully navigate their recruiting journeys, receive multiple offers, and earn lucrative scholarships! To help you on this journey I have provided both a downloadable copy of what is in this book and a blank version of all templates I used. You can go to ScoreCollegeScholarships.com and click on Templates.

Good Luck!

SECTION I: **ARGUING FOR AN INTENTIONAL RECRUITING PROCESS**

INTRODUCTION

According to the National Federation of State High School Association's (NFHS) latest records, 7.8 million high school students currently participate in athletics. Of that total, nearly 2 million of the students pursue recruiting by colleges to some extent. Incredibly, these statistics have increased for twenty-five consecutive years![1] Many high school students play sports and pursue collegiate athletics.

Only 6%, or 480,000 high school athletes, however, currently compete in National Collegiate Athletic Association (NCAA) sports in college at any level, including Division I, II, and III. Becoming a collegiate athlete is not easy based on the small percentage of high school athletes that compete in college. Most high school athletes choose not to pursue collegiate athletics, and those that do may not get the opportunity to participate.

The NCAA compiled the following chart in 2016 based on the *2014-15 High School Athletics Participation Survey* conducted by the NFHS and the NCAA's *Sports Sponsorship and Participation Rates Report*. The table illustrates the percent of high school athletes competing in college by gender and by sport:[2]

HIGH SCHOOL ATHLETES COMPETING IN COLLEGE

	High School Participants	NCAA Participants	Overall % HS to NCAA	% HS to NCAA Division I	% HS to NCAA Division II	% HS to NCAA Division III
Men						
Baseball	486,567	34,198	7.0%	2.1%	2.2%	2.7%
Basketball	541,479	18,697	3.5%	1.0%	1.0%	1.4%
Cross Country	250,981	14,330	5.7%	1.9%	1.4%	2.3%
Football	1,083,617	72,788	6.7%	2.6%	1.8%	2.4%
Golf	148,823	8,654	5.8%	2.0%	1.7%	2.1%
Ice Hockey	35,875	4,071	11.3%	4.6%	0.5%	6.3%
Lacrosse	108,450	13,165	12.1%	2.9%	2.2%	7.1%
Soccer	432,569	24,477	5.7%	1.3%	1.5%	2.8%
Swimming	137,087	9,715	7.1%	2.8%	1.1%	3.2%
Tennis	157,240	8,211	5.2%	1.7%	1.1%	2.4%
Track & Field	578,632	28,177	4.9%	1.9%	1.2%	1.7%
Volleyball	54,418	1,818	3.3%	0.7%	0.8%	1.8%
Water Polo	21,626	1,044	4.8%	2.6%	0.7%	1.5%
Wrestling	258,208	7,049	2.7%	1.0%	0.7%	1.0%
Women						
Basketball	429,504	16,589	3.9%	1.2%	1.1%	1.6%
Cross Country	221,616	16,150	7.3%	2.7%	1.7%	2.8%
Field Hockey	60,549	5,894	9.7%	2.9%	1.2%	5.7%
Golf	72,582	5,221	7.2%	3.0%	2.1%	2.1%
Ice Hockey	9,418	2,175	23.1%	9.0%	1.1%	13.1%
Lacrosse	84,785	10,994	13.0%	3.7%	2.5%	6.7%

Soccer	375,681	26,995	7.2%	2.4%	1.9%	2.9%
Softball	364,103	19,628	5.4%	1.7%	1.6%	2.1%
Swimming	166,838	12,428	7.4%	3.2%	1.1%	3.1%
Tennis	182,876	8,960	4.9%	1.6%	1.1%	2.2%
Track & Field	478,726	28,797	6.0%	2.7%	1.5%	1.8%
Volleyball	432,176	17,026	3.9%	1.2%	1.2%	1.6%
Water Polo	19,204	1,152	6.0%	3.5%	1.1%	1.4%

Sources: *High school figures from the 2014-15 High School Athletics Participation Survey conducted by the National Federation of State High School Associations. College numbers from the NCAA Sports Sponsorship and Participation Rates Report.*

The chances of competing in your chosen sport at a college or university are not high. For high school seniors wanting to pursue an NCAA-sponsored sport, the prospects range from a high of 23.1% in women's ice hockey to a low of 2.7% in men's wrestling. These figures do not take into account the opportunities that are available to compete in the National Association of Intercollegiate Athletics (NAIA) and National Junior College Athletic Association (NJCAA). But factoring in those statistics does not change the overall picture much — it is still a huge uphill battle to transition from a high school athlete to a college one.

Unwavering desire and hard work may yield success, but those qualities cannot guarantee it. In sports, nothing is ever assured. Pursuing sports constitutes a gamble competitive athletics are high risk, high reward. Prospective student-athletes immerse themselves in their sport and put themselves in the recruiting pipeline with no assurance that they will ever reap the rewards of their efforts.

Furthermore, according to the NCAA, up to one-in-four athletes participating at the collegiate level eventually drop their sport before graduating from a college or university.[3] Athletes drop out of competition because they cannot compete at the level expected, do not like their college coach or teammates, or lose interest in the sport. In effect, what they experience once they get to college is not what they expected academically, athletically, or socially — the experience ended up being a poor fit.

Getting recruited and finding the right fit can be challenging for students because there is no way to practice or gain experience before beginning. Like buying your first car, embarking on the recruiting trail leaves you wondering what to do and how to do it. But unlike buying a car, that you may do several times in your lifetime, you will only go through the collegiate recruiting process once. Therefore, it is hard to draw from experience.

The recruiting process itself also makes finding the right fit challenging. Coaches have limited staffs and time. Coaches also primarily focus on the upcoming recruiting class, which compresses the timeframe within which to make contacts, evaluate recruits, and determine to whom to make official recruiting visit invitations and offers.

As a middle school or high school student, how do you know what represents the right fit and your "best" opportunity? Your "best" opportunity may be the best academic school you can get into and still play your sport. "Best" may be playing for the highest-ranked team in your sport that's based at a decent school. It may mean attending a program where you can fulfill goals as a student-athlete "best" suited to your expectations.

English philosopher and politician Francis Bacon once proclaimed: "Hope is a good breakfast but a bad supper." While being hopeful yields a more positive state of mind, prospective student-athletes need more than optimism to be recruited at the next level. Undertake every step of your recruiting process with *intention* — intention to find the best opportunity for you. Moreover, if you put in countless hours honing your skills at a sport to be considered at the collegiate level, you should invest time into the process for getting into a school and onto a team that works best for you. After all of the training, all of the practices, and all of the competitions and travel, you deserve to discover your *best* opportunity.

This book combines information pulled together from various sources and personal experience to provide a helpful one-stop resource. These pages will take you step-by-step through the collegiate athletic recruiting process — the highs and lows, the expectations, and the surprises, so you can pursue what makes sense and avoid some of the pitfalls I encountered. You may choose to follow the proven methodology step-by-step or simply reference individual topics in the table of contents about which you would like to know more.

At the culmination of my recruiting process, a college coach graciously wrote the following email:

From: [Coach]
Date: October 25, 2016 at 5:18:23 PM PDT
To: "Laura Dickinson '17"
Subject: Re: Recruiting Process and Application
Timing Update

Hi Laura,

Thank you for the way you handled your college process. You have been nothing short of amazing. If I could give a seminar for other prospective students I would make you the model. I must believe [Selected School] sees all that we do and they will make certain of a good outcome. You will make an outstanding addition to their program. I am sad I won't get to coach you in college but happy you found a home.

We wish you all the best.

[Coach]

While I had an offer from this coach, I didn't end up with his program. Nevertheless, I am pleased that I conducted nearly every step of my recruiting process with *intention*.

The recruiting process takes time, discipline, and organization. I hope you experience similar success and find the best fit to fulfill your dreams of participating in collegiate athletics.

KEY SUMMARY POINTS:

›   Only 6% of high school athletes compete at the collegiate level.

›   Following a structured, disciplined, and intentional recruiting process will put you on the radar of college coaches and uncover your best collegiate athletic opportunities.

SECTION II: **REFLECTING, RESEARCHING, AND EVALUATING**

CHAPTER 1: **PERSONAL REFLECTIONS**

Over the course of several years, you have refined your craft – playing a sport for national teams, club teams, and/or your high school, traveling far and wide to compete against top-flight competitors, rolling out of bed early mornings to attend practice, and studying late nights to keep up with homework. What could be better than rewarding all of that commitment and hard work by competing as a collegiate athlete?

Up to 7.8 million high school athletes may contemplate this dream each year. Living away from home for the first time, stepping-up to the rigors of a college curriculum, and competing at a higher level give many of these athletes pause — and rightly so. Playing a sport in college represents a tremendous commitment fraught with sacrifices that athletes performing at a high level know all too well.

Before embarking on the process of pursuing collegiate athletics, a prospective student-athlete should reflect and consider the following questions:

> **What is your motivation to pursue athletics in college?**

If you are passionate about your sport, want it to dictate your college lifestyle, and are driven by a desire to do this for yourself, then becoming a collegiate athlete remains a possibility. If you pursue a sport to satisfy your parents' or someone else's expectations, then consider if you are truly motivated. If your heart is not behind competing in college — and you're not pursuing athletics for the right reasons — you will end up becoming unhappy, waver about quitting, or even transfer schools.

> **How committed are you to your sport?**

Inventory how much time you dedicate to your sport now, and how much you would consider dedicating to it in college. For many athletes, the level of commitment is higher in college, depending on the coach or program. While the NCAA limits in-season practice to twenty hours per week, off-hours work in the weight room and videotape review of your technique and upcoming competition add to the level of commitment required of a collegiate athlete. According to Peter Jacobs, news editor at *Business Insider* and Ivy League blogs: "the average amount of time a college athlete spends practicing is about thirty-eight hours a week for male sports and thirty-three hours for female sports."[4]

> **What is your level of work ethic?**

The NCAA requires minimum grade point averages and course units to remain eligible to participate in athletics. Coaches of some individual programs require grade point averages of their athletes above the NCAA minimum. Some colleges stipulate mandatory study hall hours for athletes. Work effort in college will far exceed what high school requires. Attending every class, paying attention, taking notes, studying harder, and asking for help are hallmarks of a greater academic work ethic in college, especially if you are a student-athlete.

› **What are your other interests in college?**

College may represent a time to try new experiences, like serving on student government, volunteering, or studying abroad. If you are fully committed to collegiate athletics, it may be harder to pursue other interests on campus. Be sure you are ready to commit the majority of your time to the pursuit of your sport.

› **What are the athletic options available to you?**

Many colleges and universities offer club teams and intramurals, which represent an outlet for athletes interested in continuing their sport, but who may not be willing to make the commitment to collegiate athletics. For other sports, like swimming and cross-country, numerous opportunities exist on college campuses to work out without competing.

› **Do the benefits of playing college sports outweigh the level of commitment required?**

Benefits vary by school, but some collegiate athletes obtain scholarships, free equipment, free food, the opportunity to sign-up for classes before other students, and assignment extensions. At the same time, you may wake up before 5:00 a.m. for practice and spend days eating, sleeping, working out, and studying with few opportunities to socialize. The trade-offs represent a personal decision.

Based on my recruiting and collegiate experience to date, I offer the following advice if you are considering athletics in college:

› **Don't underestimate potential options.**

Before entering the recruiting process, you won't know what you don't know. This book walks you through an intentional process that uncovers options you may not have thought possible. Division II and Division III colleges offer countless options for student-athletes. Despite having Division I options, I ended up enrolling in a Division III school.

> **Playing collegiate athletics can ease the transition to college.**

Think about it. One of your greatest concerns about going to college may be that you won't know anyone. How will you make new friends? One of the best ways to ease the transition to college is to start the experience with a built-in social circle — your teammates. These will be people with whom you associate for up to twenty hours or more per week. Some teammates may even be roommates. How wonderful would it be to have friends with the same athletic interest among all grade levels ready to accept you? Some college teammates can become life-long friends. This potential benefit underscores the importance of evaluating your prospective teammates carefully on official recruiting visits (see Chapter 19, Official Recruiting Visits).

> **Being a college athlete contributes to your education.**

Playing a sport in college focuses your priorities, forces you to organize your time, and gives you an outlet for working off the rigors of college academic demands. Different athletic experiences can be applied in the classroom and to the working world. Prospective employers may be impressed with the level of commitment you maintain as a collegiate athlete.

> **The exhilaration of college athletics can be unmatched.**

You get to represent your college, compete for your team, and work with an accomplished coaching staff. Such an environment can help you reach your athletic potential. When you get introduced at your first game, match, or meet in college, the euphoria you feel will likely far exceed anything you experience in high school or club sports.

Take a moment to reflect about these questions and thoughts. At the end of your reflection, you should be able to write down a statement answering why you want to compete as a collegiate athlete.

Now that you have reflected on your motivations to pursue participating in collegiate athletics, it's time to begin an organized and deliberate research effort about prospective schools and teams.

KEY SUMMARY POINTS:

› Before embarking on a recruiting process, ask the question "Why?" Why do you want to participate in collegiate athletics?

› How well do your expectations for college and level of commitment match the demands of competing as a collegiate athlete?

CHAPTER 2: **VENN DIAGRAM FOR RESEARCH**

Before beginning the daunting task of figuring out which programs to pursue and whether a collegiate coach would even be interested in my athletic ability, I needed a way to organize the information I would research and compile.

A Venn diagram, also known as a logic diagram or a set diagram, depicts the relationships among a limited collection of various sets. Some people associate the MasterCard symbol of partially overlapping orange and yellow circles with a Venn diagram. To research different facets of collegiate athletic recruiting, I think of a Venn diagram with three intersecting circles. Each circle represents an important aspect of making the momentous decision of where to participate in collegiate athletics for any prospective student-athlete. The first circle features "Academic Qualifications," the second circle involves "Athletic Qualifications," and the third circle encompasses "Expectations and Fit."

Venn Diagram for Collegiate
Athletic Recruiting

By collecting facts and information about colleges or universities you may be considering, you will not only determine how strong a school is academically, but whether your academic qualifications measure up to admissions standards. Athletic qualifications will not only quantify how good the team is at a school in the sport you are pursuing, but how well you can make contributions to that team and how likely a coach is to recruit you. Finally, "Expectations and Fit" inform how good a match the school and team may be for your expectations.

"Academic Qualifications" determine the academic profile of a college or university, and how well your academic credentials measure up to admissions expectations. Rankings, yield (i.e., the percent of admitted students that enroll), and other statistics from news publications and websites can be used to quantify the relative reputation of a college or university. Average grade points and standardized test scores for students that a school admits can be used to inform the academic quality of a school's student population. When comparing a school's statistics to grade point average and standardized test scores, a recruit can determine how realistic gaining admission to the school may be. Specific references to college search tools where a determination can be further informed are also incorporated. Chapter 3 details specific metrics, data, and sources used to stipulate academic credentials.

At the conclusion of researching and making comparisons about academic qualifications, a prospective student-athlete will be able to sort colleges and universities that he or she is considering into "reach," "likely," and "safety" designations. A "reach" involves a school where gaining admission will be challenging. Some highly sought-after colleges and universities constitute a reach for *all* applying students. A "likely" college or university represents a school where a recruit stands a decent chance, usually better than 50-50, of gaining admission. A "safety" school represents a college or university where a recruit falls well above the 75th percentile for grade point average and standardized test scores of accepted students. Regardless of the number of schools you pursue for recruiting and to which you may eventually apply, the number of "reach," "likely," and "safety" designations should be allocated roughly into one-third each. That way, a candidate improves the odds of getting into at least one school and diversifies the odds of having a range of options.

"Athletic Qualifications" quantify how good a team is in the sport you are pursuing at a given school, how well you can make contributions to that team, and how likely a coach is to pursue you. Athletic research entails compiling factual information about a team, its league, and recruiting requirements, and the extent to which a recruit's athletic ability matches a team's needs and expectations. Data and metrics compiled will vary by sport. This book provides a particular example used for competitive swimming, which is my sport, and the steps that can be taken to customize research for your selected sport. Chapter 4 offers specific metrics, data, and sources used to stipulate athletic qualifications.

"Expectations and Fit" outlines how well the college or university and athletic team may match your expectations. This set of information represents the most open-ended aspect of the research. Examples of criteria for the fit of a college or university include geography, setting, enrollment size, and type of school, among others. Examples of criteria for the fit of the team include practice hours per week, co-ed vs. single-sex workouts, and facilities, among others. A prospective student-athlete should draw from reflections in Chapter 1 to see whether the subjective criteria involving a school and program match personal expectations. Chapter 5 lists a sample set of metrics, data, and sources used to inform expectations and fit.

While the circles pictured in the Venn diagram depict the same size, you may choose to emphasize one of the three categories more than the others. You may also elect to include an additional dimension of your research, such as affordability.

You will also notice that the circles in the Venn diagram overlap. As you dig deeper into your research, you may discover a college or university that meets your academic expectations where you stand a solid chance of gaining admission, but one with an athletic team that does not match your capabilities. Likewise, you may discover a college or university with a team that represents an outstanding match for your athletic expectations, but does not match your academic goals and capabilities. The point of conducting research and performing due diligence is to make sure you are identifying potential opportunities that fulfill your expectations for academics, athletics, *and* fit. At the conclusion of your research, you should be able to array where different schools fall on your Venn diagram. Example provided.

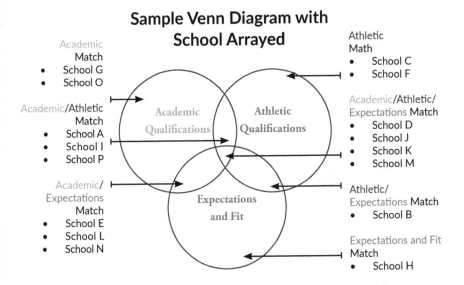

Sample Venn Diagram with School Arrayed

Academic
Match
- School G
- School O

Academic/Athletic
Match
- School A
- School I
- School P

Academic/
Expectations
Match
- School E
- School L
- School N

Academic
Qualifications

Athletic
Qualifications

Expectations
and Fit

Athletic
Math
- School C
- School F

Academic/Athletic/
Expectations Match
- School D
- School J
- School K
- School M

Athletic/
Expectations Match
- School B

Expectations and Fit
Match
- School H

One of the most important things to do throughout your recruiting process is to document everything. A research database using an Excel or similar spreadsheet can help document and organize information. First of all, you cannot possibly remember the myriad of data you come across over the span of several months to even a couple of years. Second, data exists scattered across multiple sources. Third, data gets uncovered at various points in time; you will learn some information upfront from initial research while prospective coaches and teammates convey other information during an official recruiting visit.

A research database becomes the repository into which relevant information gets compiled. Your research database will be the basis for evaluating tradeoffs among recruiting options. Consistent with the Venn diagram, divide the research database into three sections: "Academic Qualifications," "Athletic Qualifications," and "Expectations and Fit." You will add sub-headings to different sections as you learn new information. Each of these categories is detailed with corresponding metrics in subsequent chapters:

"Academics Qualifications" in Chapter 3, "Athletic Qualifications" in Chapter 4, and "Expectations and Fit" in Chapter 5. Data for each metric informs schools being evaluated. I also provide examples of corresponding metrics from my research database. With this roadmap for conducting research, let's get started by compiling data and metrics about "Academic Qualifications."

KEY SUMMARY POINTS:

> A framework with three components — academic qualifications, athletic qualifications, and expectations and fit — can help you evaluate a college or university and its athletic program for your sport.

> Detailed research will inform which schools to pursue and to what extent a coach will be interested in recruiting you.

> A spreadsheet should be populated with data for various metrics to inform tradeoffs among schools and recruiting options.

CHAPTER 3: **ACADEMIC QUALIFICATIONS**

"Academic Qualifications" determine how strong a school is educationally and whether your academic credentials measure up to admissions standards.

A plethora of information about a school's admissions process and rankings along with other statistics can be compiled to determine the requirements for a school, how strong a school is academically, and your chances of getting admitted. While not all information will be available at a high school-specific level — for instance, the average grade point average for students from your high school admitted to a particular college — every effort should be made to compile relevant data for your research.

Information about application types accepted, details about standardized test administration, and the number of recommendations required and allowed can be found on college or university websites themselves under the header "Admissions." College guides, including *Peterson's Four-Year Colleges, Barron's Profiles of American Colleges,* and *Fiske Guide to Colleges* also feature academic qualifications and admissions requirements. Other sources for relevant research data may be used as well. If you compile conflicting information, always defer to the college or university's website. Sometimes these requirements change annually, so be sure to identify whether the information you are collecting is specific to your year of admission.

Because you will be entering information into a spreadsheet, and adding to it as information becomes available over time, begin by labeling your spreadsheet with "Recruiting Database" and the heading "Academic Qualifications." Next, list any "Colleges or Universities" you would like to research or consider. For each college or university, the following list details information to collect (i.e., headings in your spreadsheet), the metric used to quantify that information as appropriate, specific entries to make into your spreadsheet by school, and the source of the data (i.e., how to collect the information). In my illustrative research database, "Academic Qualifications" contains four sub-headings: "Admissions Requirements," "Academic Reputation," "Admissions Qualifications," and "Admissions Chances."

WHAT DOES THE COLLEGE OR UNIVERSITY REQUIRE FOR ADMISSION?

Under the heading "Academic Qualifications," enter the sub-heading "Admissions Requirements."

> **High School Academic Program (Recommended/Required)**

According to the National Association for College Admission Counseling's (NACAC) *State of College Admissions 2015* study, 87% of college admissions representatives believe that the strength of curriculum is "considerably" or "moderately important" to a college application.[5] Many major colleges and universities, especially elite schools, expect a student to pursue a rigorous academic course load across relevant academic subjects in high school. The metric for this evaluation is whether a student fulfills a certain number of years of course work throughout his or her high school career. For these entries, indicate "Recommended" or "Required" by college in your research database. In my experience, "Recommended" usually means "Required" to put forward the strongest academic schedule and application for a college.

Even though an applicant applies to college before completing his or her senior year of high school, colleges will ask for the courses planned or underway during senior year and request a mid-year report on how well you performed through the first term of your senior year.

Here is the data to research which become headings and entries in your research database.

○ **English (Number of Years)**

Enter the number of high school years in English/language arts a given college or university recommends or requires.

○ **Math (Number of Years)**

Enter the number of high school years in mathematics a given college or university recommends or requires.

○ **Science (Number of Years)**

Enter the number of high school years in science a given college or university recommends or requires.

○ **Social Sciences/Social Studies/History (Number of Years)**

Enter the number of high school years in social sciences/ social studies/history a given college or university recommends or requires. Some schools use the broader social sciences or social studies category to include government, psychology, economics, and other courses.

○ **Foreign Language (Number of Years)**

Enter the number of high school years in foreign language a given college or university recommends or requires. Many colleges expect that the number of years be completed in the same foreign language.

○ **Art (Number of Years)**

Enter the number of high school years in art a given college or university recommends or requires. Few colleges make this stipulation, but application to the University of California campuses requires one year of high school art in the same subject or medium.

○ **Other (Specify: / Number of Years)**

Enter additional subject(s) and the number of years required.

Many colleges prefer that prospective students have the following qualifications: four years of English/language arts; four years of mathematics; three years of social sciences/social studies/history; three years of science; two years of foreign language; and up to one year of art. However, keep in mind that expectations vary by school. Harvard University and Georgia Tech, for example, recommend four years of science. Middlebury College, for example, recommends four years of the same foreign language.

Some high schools require certain courses to graduate that may not fit into specified subject categories, including: religious studies, physical education, and wellness, among others. The fact that these courses do not fit into specified category requirements limits flexibility. Start your research early in your high school career to satisfy graduation requirements. Based on my experience, I recommend mapping out your high school program at the beginning of your freshman year.

Depicted is a sample high school schedule reflecting the types of courses that I needed to complete to meet high school graduation requirements:

Required High School Schedule

Subject (Semesters)	Freshman Semester 1	Semester 2	Sophomore Semester 1	Semester 2	Junior Semester 1	Semester 2	Senior Semester 1	Semester 2
English (8)	English	English	English	English	English	English	English	English
Religious Studies (7)		Religious Studies	Religious Studies	Religious Studies	Religious Studies	Religious Studies	Religious Studies	Religious Studies
Math (8)	Math	Math	Math	Math	Math	Math	Math recommended	Math recommended
Social Science (6)	World History	World History	World History		U.S. History	U.S. History	Social Science	
Science (6)	Biology	Biology	Chemistry	Chemistry			Science recommended	Science recommended
Language (6)	Foreign Language	Foreign Language	Foreign Language	Foreign Language	Foreign Language recommended	Foreign Language recommended		
Fine Arts (2)					Art	Art		
PE (2)	PE			PE				
Courses	6	6	6	6	6	6	5	4

Graduation requirements:
English – 8 semesters
Religious studies – 7 semesters
Math – 6 semesters (8 semesters recommended)
Social science – 6 semesters
Science – 4 semesters (6 semesters recommended)

Language – 4 semesters of same language (6 semesters recommended)
Fine Arts – 2 semesters
PE – 2 semesters
College prep electives – 9 semesters
Community service and social justice
6 courses per semester

Graduation requirements appear at the bottom of the table. Fulfilling the number of semesters required or recommended for each subject at my high school, including taking six courses each semester, leaves a student with three available slots for additional Advanced Placement courses or electives.

You will want to map out a tentative four-year plan to ascertain the requirements expected and degree of flexibility in your high school schedule. Depicted is a sample high school schedule representing courses I projected taking throughout my high school career based on requirements, an interest in pursuing as rigorous a course load as my high school would allow, and an interest in doubling up on foreign language:

Projected High School Schedule

	Freshman		Sophomore		Junior		Senior		HS Tot Req or Rec	College Max Rec
	Semester 1	Semester 2	Semester 1	Semester 2	Semester 1	Semester 2	Semester 1	Semester 2		
English	English 100	English 100	English 203 Honors (1203)	English 203 Honors (1203)	English 300-399 Honors	English 300-399 Honors	English Lit & Composition 403 AP (1403)	English Lit & Composition 403 AP (1403)	8-8	8-8
								English 480		
Religious Studies		RS 100	RS 200 (8200)	RS 200 (8200)	RS 300 (8300)	RS 300 (8300)	RS 460 Sexuality	RS 400 The Path to Faith	7-7	7-0
Math	Algebra 2 Honors (2110)	Algebra 2 Honors (2110)	Geometry Honors (2200)	Geometry Honors (2200)	Pre-Calculus Honors (2313)	Pre-Calculus Honors (2313)	Calculus AP BC (2423)	Calculus AP BC (2423)	8-8	8-8
Social Science	World History I	World History I	World History II			U.S. History AP (5303)	U.S. History AP (5303)	AP Gov't and Politics (B) (5403)		6-6	6-6
Science	Biology	Biology			Chemistry	Chemistry	Physics Honors (3044)	Physics Honors (3044)	6-6	6-8
Language	French 3 Honors (4033)	French 3 Honors (4033)	French 4 AP (4043)	French 4 AP (4043)					8-8	8-8
			Spanish 2 Honors (4123)	Spanish 2 Honors (4123)	Spanish 3 Honors (4133)	Spanish 3 Honors (4133)				
Fine Arts							Studio Art A (6120)	Studio Art B (6123)	2-2	2-2
PE	PE 110				PE 713 (7713)					2-2	2-0
Courses	6	6	6	6	6	6	6	6		

The far right-hand column lists the maximum number of high school years, converted to semesters, recommended by any college. This exercise provides a roadmap for determining whether you will fulfill high school graduation requirements and position yourself for college applications with a robust academic course load. While I deviated slightly from this forecast, it helped me realize that, with religious studies and art requirements at my high school factored in, I had few options to explore electives if I was to fulfill the number of years by subject expected of most colleges and universities.

If you find yourself in such a situation, plan early, plan ahead, and understand what academic course load to pursue. Keep as many doors open down the road as possible.

WHAT TYPES OF APPLICATIONS ACCEPTED?

Continuing under "Admissions Requirements," identify which application types a college accepts for admission. As of this writing, three major types of applications exist: The Common Application, the Coalition Application, and customized applications. Standardized applications, including the Common Application and Coalition Application, may be used to enter information one-time and then apply to multiple colleges without having to repeat details for each college on your target list. Standardized applications also allow you to track important deadlines and view application progress for any one school.

> **Common Application Accepted (Yes/No)**

The Common Application is a not-for-profit organization that serves students and member institutions by providing an admissions platform for prospective students to compile and submit college applications. As of this writing, the Common Application allows access to admissions for approximately 700 colleges and universities around the world. Some schools use the Common Application exclusively, whereas other schools accept the Common Application and other application formats. For this research database entry, submit "Yes" ("Y") or "No" ("N") based on whether the college or university accepts the Common Application.

> **Coalition Application Accepted (Yes/No)**

Known as the Coalition for Access and Affordability, the Coalition Application began in 2016 and serves 90 colleges or universities, as of this writing. Like the Common Application, the Coalition Application allows information to be entered one-time, saved, and then used to apply for multiple schools. Unlike the Common Application, the Coalition Application requires the entry of individual courses and grades. For this research database entry, submit "Yes" ("Y") or "No" ("N") based on whether the college or university accepts the Coalition Application.

> **Custom Application Required (Yes/No)**

Some schools stipulate that their custom application be used exclusively to apply for admission. For example, Georgetown University refuses to use the Common Application and requires prospective students to use its own application. Regarding this, Dean of Undergraduate Admissions Charles Deacon says: "It's what keeps our pool down a little bit because we don't have the frivolous applicants."[6] For this research database entry, submit "Yes" ("Y") or "No" ("N") based on whether the college or university accepts or requires a custom application for admission.

> **Other (Explain)**

If you encounter other application platforms or expectations for a given school, make these entries in the research database under the "Other" heading. Information to list under "Other" includes whether the school accepts the following application cycles: Early Decision I ("ED1"), Early Decision II ("EDII"), Restrictive Early or Single-Choice Action ("REA"), or Early Action ("EA"). The different ways for a prospective student to apply are discussed in Chapter 20: Recruiting Tactics by Coaches and Chapter 26: Prioritizing Schools and Programs.

Upon compiling this information, discern how many different types of applications you will need to fill out based on the schools to which you apply. In my case, I learned the software and instructions for five different application formats, filling out the Common Application, Coalition Application, and three custom applications — all so I could apply to nine different schools. If you end up applying to fewer schools or are fortunate enough to apply only to schools that use the same application type, you may only have to learn one application format.

STANDARDIZED TEST ADMINISTRATION

In the *NACAC State of College Admissions 2015* study, 88.2% of college admissions representatives believed that standardized admission test results were "considerably" or "moderately important" to a college application.[7] "Standardized Test Administration," another aspect of "Admissions Requirements," specifies what a college or university expects about which standardized test scores may be submitted, the scope of standardized tests taken, special rules that may apply about scoring, and whether submission of all test scores is required to consider an applicant:

› **Tests Accepted (SAT/ACT/Other)**

Colleges and universities consider three major types of tests for entrance: the Scholastic Aptitude Test (SAT), American College Testing (ACT), and International Baccalaureate (IB) exams. Whereas most schools accept either the SAT or ACT (i.e., both), some schools prefer one test or the other, and a select few only take one of the standardized tests. If a school accepts both the SAT and ACT, you only have to take one or the other. For this research database entry, specify "SAT" for a school that only accepts the SAT, "ACT" for a school that only takes the ACT, "SAT/ACT" for a school that accepts either test, and "Other" for a school that welcomes an additional test. Be sure to specify other approved tests.

› **Test-Optional (Yes/No)**

Increasingly, admissions offices at a growing number of colleges and universities are test-optional; that is, their college application does not require submission of standardized test scores. In some cases, submission of test scores is highly encouraged, but not required. Bowdoin College in Brunswick, Maine and Wake Forest University in Winston-Salem, North Carolina represent two examples of test- optional schools. Over 850 colleges and universities, as of this writing, now fall into the test-optional category. For a complete list of schools, consult The National Center for Fair and Open Testing at fairtest.org/university/optional. For the "Test-Optional" research database entry, specify "Yes" ("Y") for a school that is test-optional and "No" ("N") for a school that is not test-optional.

> **TOEFL/IELTS Required (Yes/No/Recommended)**

TOEFL stands for Test of English as a foreign language. IELTS stands for International English Language Testing System. Whereas the TOEFL and IELTS test academic English, IELTS also offers a more general test of English proficiency. For this research database entry, specify "Yes" ("Y") for a school that requires a test for those where English is not the first language, "No" ("N") where either test is not required, and "Recommended" where either test is encouraged but not required.

> **Test Essay Required (Yes/No/Recommended).**

When registering for standardized tests, a high school student may elect "SAT with Essay" or "ACT with Essay." Admissions offices of some colleges and universities require the essay portion of the SAT or ACT. If you complete the "SAT with Essay" or "ACT with Essay," you will be able to apply to colleges and universities that require the essay. For this research database entry, specify "Yes" ("Y") for a school that requires an essay with the standardized test, "No" ("N") for a college or university that does not require an essay, and "Recommended" for a school that encourages but does not require including the essay portion of the standardized test.

> **SAT Subject Tests (Required/Recommended/Number)**

According to the College Board that administers SAT Subject Tests (often referred to as SAT II Tests), such tests are "college admission exams on [individual academic] subjects that you choose to best showcase your strengths and interests."[8] As of this writing, there are 20 different SAT Subject tests, including:

- Mathematics:
  - Math Level 1
  - Math Level 2
- Science:
  - Biology
  - Chemistry
  - Physics
- English:
  - Literature
- History:
  - U.S. History
  - World History
- Languages:
  - Spanish
  - Spanish with Listening
  - French
  - French with Listening
  - Chinese with Listening
  - Italian
  - German
  - German with Listening
  - Modern Hebrew
  - Latin
  - Japanese with Listening
  - Korean with Listening

Selective and elite colleges and universities often stipulate an SAT Subject Test as part of an application. Some schools recommend taking two subject tests while a handful of schools expect three tests for admission. A few schools request only subject tests if an applicant submits the SAT for his or her standardized test and not the ACT. Keep in mind that "Recommended" usually means "Required" to put forward your strongest standardized test results for college. I know of no colleges or universities that specify which subject to take for general applications, unless you are applying to a particular program within their institution (e.g., Math Level II for engineering and select business programs). For this research database entry, enter "Required," "Recommended," "Optional," or "Not Required" for a given school, and the number of subject tests desired.

I suggest taking SAT Subject Tests as soon as you complete high school coursework relating to that topic while the material is still fresh in your mind. Avoid waiting to start taking tests. When I completed a French 4 AP course in my sophomore year of high school, I took the corresponding SAT Subject Test that spring. If I had waited until the time when most students take standardized tests — typically starting in the spring of junior year — I might have forgotten a significant amount of vocabulary and material. The other advantage of taking SAT Subject Tests right after you complete academic coursework is that it spreads out the number of standardized tests you have to take in a compressed and busy spring of junior year and beginning of senior year, when college applications and official recruiting visits converge. Of note, not all SAT Subject Test scores have to be reported, unless a college or university requires that you submit all standardized test scores.

› **Super-Scoring (SAT/ACT/Either/No)**

If an applicant takes multiple SAT or ACT tests, some colleges will super-score the results, also known as the Flexible Testing Option. Super-scoring means accepting the best result for a given sub-category on any equivalent test taken. The SAT includes reading comprehension (i.e., verbal), math, an optional writing/essay section, and an overall score. The ACT includes individual scores for English, math, reading comprehension, science, and an optional writing section for those taking the essay portion of the test. Math and science scores get combined to form a STEM score. Combining English, reading, and writing scores generates an English/language arts (ELA) score. Scores from the individual subjects produce an overall composite score for the test-taker. If, for example, you complete the ACT twice, and the results are higher for math on the first exam, science on the second exam, English on the first exam, and reading comprehension on the second exam, then a college that super-scores will cherry-pick the best results to form a higher overall test result based on the two exams. Some schools will only super-score the SAT or ACT, while others will super-score multiple results from either test. No school of which I am aware combines scores across the SAT and ACT; that is, a school will not take the verbal score from an SAT and combine it with the math result from an ACT exam. The College Board (the administrator of the SAT) and ACT (the non-profit that administers the ACT test) will allow students to submit to a college whichever test scores they choose, but not individual parts of a scored exam. For this research database entry, enter "SAT" if a given school super-scores the SAT, "ACT" if it super-scores that exam, "SAT/ACT" or "Either" if it will do it for one or the other, and "No" ("N") if a school will not super-score either exam.

> **All Test Scores Required (Yes/Recommended/No)**

Some colleges or universities require that an applicant submits all test scores taken, regardless of the results. Many indicate that poor test results will not put an applicant at a disadvantage. Others indicate that multiple test results should be provided for super-scoring to take place. For this research database entry, specify "Yes" ("Y") for a school that requires submission of all test scores, "Recommended," or "No" ("N") for a school that does not require all test scores.

RECOMMENDATIONS

The final aspect of "Admissions Requirements" involves recommendations. Over time, recommendations from counselors, teachers, coaches, pastors, and family friends — while still essential — have become less and less important in the college application process. Only 59% of college admissions respondents in the *NACAC State of College Admissions 2015* survey believed that "teacher and counselor recommendations" were either "considerably" or "moderately important."[9] Some schools, like the University of California system and the University of Washington, do not require any recommendations. "Recommendations" represent a category of research database headings involving what a college or university expects about the number and type of recommendations that should be submitted with your application:

> **High School Counselor (Yes/No)**

Every college or university I researched that requires one or more recommendations requires a recommendation on an applicant's behalf from a high school counselor. Some high schools assign "academic" and "college" counselors to each student. Also, your high school counselor will submit a midyear report to colleges to which you have applied after the first term of your senior year. In this regard, it is imperative to develop a strong and personal relationship(s) with your counselor(s) from the beginning of your high school career. For this research database entry, specify "Yes" ("Y") for a school that requires submission of a recommendation from a high school counselor and "No" ("N") for a school that does not.

> **Teacher 1 (Yes/No)**

Most schools require at least one recommendation from a teacher from whom you have taken a course. It will be important to select a teacher who knows you well — ideally in and out of the classroom — with the ability to speak to your intellectual curiosity and contributions to high school. The person writing the recommendation may or may not be a teacher in whose class you received an "A." I got my recommendation from an English teacher from whom I took two courses, and whose daughter competed on the high school athletic team I captained; as a result, the teacher knew me well in and out of the classroom. Enter "Yes" ("Y") when at least one teacher recommendation is required. Enter "No" ("N") when no teacher recommendation is required.

> **Teacher 2 (Yes/No)**

Many schools require a second teacher recommendation. Enter "Yes" ("Y") when a second recommendation is required and "No" ("N") when it is not.

> **Criteria (Junior/Senior Year only, Academic Subjects only)**

Some colleges and universities stipulate that a teacher recommendation must come from a teacher in a course taken during your junior or senior year of high school. This expectation makes it tough because by the time you submit college applications in November or December of your senior year, senior year teachers may not know you as well. Other schools stipulate that recommendations come from teachers in academic subjects, including English, math, science, or history. While exceptions can be made depending on the level of your interest and accomplishments in a subject, art, religious studies, and physical education teachers are usually excluded from recommendations by these schools. In my view, selecting a teacher who knows you best is the most important criterion. For this heading, enter for a given school whether recommendations must be from teachers in your "Junior/Senior Year" and whether they must be teachers in "Academic Subjects."

› **Supplemental Recommendations (Number Permitted/No)**

Some colleges and universities accommodate supplemental recommendations in their admissions process. Additional recommendations usually come from someone other than a high school counselor or teacher but may involve an extra counselor or teacher as well. Community service representatives, clergy, music teachers, and coaches often qualify. If you are a prospective student-athlete, supplemental recommendations represent the opportunity to have your national coach, club team coach, or high school coach — the mentors for whom you have been competing athletically for many, many years — write a recommendation on your behalf. For this heading in the research database, enter the number of supplemental recommendations allowed by the college or university. Most admissions officers frown on a stack of recommendation letters for an applicant; keep the number you submit limited. Enter the number (#) permitted if a school allows supplemental recommendations or "No" ("N") if a college or university does not accept additional recommendations.

> **Interviews (Yes/Recommended/Optional/Available/No)**
>
> Interviews with admissions officers or alumni represent an outstanding way to collect better information about a school and a way for prospective students to highlight the person behind the application. Some colleges require interviews (i.e., enter "Yes" or "Y"), some colleges recommend interviews ("Recommended"), some schools specify that interviews are optional ("Optional") or available ("Available"), and others do not require them at all ("No" or "N").

APPLICATION ESSAYS

Application essays represent a chance to express yourself and convey your voice to an admissions committee. A standardized application platform, like the Common Application or Coalition Application, features one essay selected among several prompts as part of the submission. Most individual colleges and universities then require additional supplemental essays to customize what they ask of a prospective student. Many schools change their essay prompts from one admissions cycle to another.

Schools release essay prompts as early as June, so at the beginning of the summer after your junior year, you can begin scouring college websites for what they expect. I highly recommend getting started on applications and essays during the summer between the junior and senior year of high school. That's because with official recruiting visits to take, college applications to submit, a challenging course load to fulfill, and senior year activities to enjoy, you're going to be busy.

One tremendous resource for identifying college application essays as they get released is *Collegeessayorganizer.com*.

This website offers either free or fee-based services for users.

Among the free services, a user can enter colleges and universities in which he or she is interested, and inventory required and optional application essay prompts. If the prompts do not appear for that application cycle, the website will send you an email indicating when a school announces its essay prompts. What could be better? Collegeessayorganizer.com also organizes and batches similar essay prompts so that you know how many "original" essays will need to be constructed for the schools selected:

› **Required (Number)**

For a given school being considered, enter the number of essays required. Be sure to include the essay(s) required in the standardized application format the school may allow.

› **Optional (Number)**

In the same way, enter the number of optional essays a school allows for inclusion in an application.

In my case, I seriously considered 18 schools at one point. While those schools required some 47 different essays, only 27 were truly unique in nature. In the end, I narrowed my list to 14 schools I seriously considered and submitted nine applications requiring 25 essays, 13 of which were unique.

By the time you've finished researching and compiling all of this information about application requirements, you will have a decent idea about what to expect during the application process; you will also have a good understanding of the differences among schools. More importantly, all the disparate information scattered across websites and publications will be in one place for you to reference and update throughout your collegiate athletic recruiting and application process.

WHAT IS THE SCHOOL'S ACADEMIC REPUTATION?

A school's academic reputation can be significant in assessing academic qualifications, and whether it is the type of school that matches your abilities. A highly-ranked school will likely draw a stronger, more academically-oriented clientele. If your study habits and track record match this type of environment, then go for it! It will be important to discern whether academic demands exceed your expectations or whether educational offerings are not challenging enough. The following metrics attempt to gauge a school's "Academic Reputation":

> **Yield (Percentage)**

Yield represents a simple calculation: the percentage of students admitted to a college or university that enrolls. If ten students get accepted by a college and only four enroll, then the school's yield is 40%. The higher the yield, the more attractive the school is and presumably the better its reputation. Yield indeed exposes what the market believes — consumers making choices among multiple options. More reputable schools achieve yields in the 70% to 80% range, like Harvard, Stanford, and Yale. Institutions with sterling reputations, however, may only generate enrolled students in the 40% range. A large basket of colleges and universities fall below a yield of 20%, even though many of them offer high-quality opportunities. Yield becomes one metric with which to divide schools into "reach" (i.e., higher yield), "likely," and "safety" (i.e., lower yield) classifications. For this heading, enter the yield percentage by school.

> ***U.S. News and World Report* Rank (Ranking/Classification)**

Over two decades ago, *U.S. News and World Report* became the first publication to statistically rank colleges and universities.

What started out as a way to attract subscribers and promote magazine sales became a full-fledged industry!

The methodology used by *U.S. News* ranks schools based on a weighting using the following criteria:

○ **22.5% Graduation and Retention Rates.**

According to the *U.S. News* publication, "the higher the proportion of first-year students who return to campus for sophomore year [of college] and eventually graduate, the better a school is apt to be at offering the classes and services that students need to succeed."[10]

○ **22.5% Undergraduate Academic Reputation.**

An academic survey conducted among university presidents, provosts, deans of admissions, and high school counselors assesses the academic reputation (e.g., faculty dedication to teaching) among peer institutions.

○ **20.0% Faculty Resources**

U.S. News combines five factors to determine the extent of faculty resources: class size, "faculty salary, the proportion of professors with the highest degrees in their fields, student-faculty ratio, and proportion of full-time faculty."[11] The publication notes that "the more satisfied students are about their contact with professors, the more they will learn and the more likely they are to graduate."[12]

○ **12.5% Student Selectivity**

This metric considers three factors: SAT and ACT composite test scores among admitted applicants, admitted applicants "that graduated in the top ten percent of their high school class," and acceptance rate (i.e., ratio of admitted applicants to total applicants).[13] *U.S. News* purports "a school's academic atmosphere is determined in part by students' abilities and ambitions."[14]

○ **10.0% Financial Resources**

Average per student spending on instruction, student services, and research reflect the breadth and quality of programs and services a college offers.

○ **7.5% Graduate Rate Performance**

This metric measures the extent to which a college's programs and services contribute to graduation rate. Spending and student populations are adjusted in order that *U.S. News* can "measure the difference between a school's six-year graduation rate... and the rate of graduation predicted for a given class."[15]

○ **5.0% Alumni Giving Rate**

Alumni giving rate measures the percentage of living alumni that make contributions to the college as an indirect indicator of student satisfaction.

While these criteria are not true measures of academic quality, each of them indirectly contributes to the educational level of an institution and students' perceptions about the quality of education they receive. See *colleges. usnews.rankingsandreviews.com/best-colleges* to source these various metrics and identify the ranking for various colleges and universities under consideration.

U.S. News segregates national universities, liberal arts colleges, regional universities, and regional colleges for its rankings. While this step provides more specificity about schools within each classification, it is much harder to compare schools across classifications. If in 2017, Princeton is ranked number one among national universities and Williams is ranked number one among liberal arts colleges, how do you compare the two? Despite this limitation in the *U.S. News* data, for purposes of a research database, enter the designation and rank for the school: "1 (Nat'l)" could be used for the number one national university, and "1 (LAC)" could be used for the number one liberal arts college.

> **Forbes Rank (Ranking)**

For the tenth year in 2017, *Forbes* magazine annually produces a college rankings list. Unlike the *U.S. News* rankings that feature both inputs (i.e., selectivity metrics; e.g., test scores, high school class rank of accepted applicants) and outputs (e.g., graduation rates), *Forbes'* rankings predominantly emphasize outputs. In effect, this survey is less interested in students that get admitted and more interested in the benefits of attending a college and which schools provide the best benefits. *Forbes* rankings combine national universities and liberal arts colleges into one survey, making it easier to compare institutions. The methodology used by *Forbes* ranks schools based on a weighting using the following criteria:

o **32.5% Post-Graduate Success**

This metric combines the salary of alumni and where established, influential, and innovative contributors to society received their degrees.

o **25.0% Student Debt**

By combining average federal student loan debt, loan default rates, and the expected vs. actual percentage of students taking federal loans, this metric assesses the affordability of matriculating at a specific college.

○ **25.0% Student Satisfaction**

Retention rates, transfers to other schools, and student satisfaction surveys objectively quantify student satisfaction.

○ **10.0% Academic Success**

Academic success measures the number of national scholarships and fellowships (e.g., Rhodes Scholars, Fulbright Scholars) earned by students at a particular school and the percent that go on to earn PhDs in any field.[16]

○ **7.5% Graduation Rate**

This metric considers the four-year graduation rate (5%) and the actual vs. predicted graduation rate (2.5%).

See *forbes.com/top-colleges/list* to review these various metrics and identify the ranking for various colleges and universities under consideration. Enter the rank for each school into your research database.

› **Niche Rank (Number)**

Niche rigorously analyzes "dozens of public data sets and millions of reviews to produce overall rankings, report cards, and profiles" for colleges.[17] The U.S. Department of Education compiles over 30 million college reviews and survey responses from college students from which rankings get generated. *Niche's* ranking methodology incorporates several weighted metrics, as follows:

○ 35.0%: Academics (e.g., acceptance rate, quality of professors)

○ 25.0%: Value (e.g., average loan amount, alumni earnings)

○ 10.0%: Professors (e.g., awards won by faculty, student-faculty ratio)

○ 7.5%: Student Life (e.g., safety, diversity, athletics)

○ 7.5%: Overall Experience (e.g., student surveys, alumni surveys)

○ 5.0%: Campus (e.g., quality of food, quality of housing)

○ 5.0%: Diversity (e.g., student body ethnic composition)

○ 2.5%: Local Area (e.g., median rent)

○ 2.5%: Safety (e.g., campus crime rate, local crime rate)

The website also provides valuable information to help prospective students sort schools. For example, colleges are ranked by state, by admission selectivity, and by GPA, SAT, and ACT scores at various intervals. *See colleges.niche.com/rankings to access the rankings and various sorts. Enter the rank for each school under consideration.*

› **High School Evaluation (Specify)**

Some high schools provide classifications of colleges and universities. For example, my high school arrays colleges and universities into: "most selective," "very selective," and "other" classifications. My high school also classifies colleges and universities by type (e.g., "private," "public," "Jesuit," "University of California," and "community college"). Ask your high school counselor for available data and enter ranks or classifications into your research database as appropriate.

› **Other College Ranking Services**

To be sure, other rankings and sources exist to profile the reputations of colleges and universities, among them:

○ *Washington Monthly College Rankings*

○ *Faculty Scholarly Productivity Rankings*

○ *Top American Research Universities*

○ *Wall Street Journal Top 50 Feeder Schools*

WHAT ARE THE ADMISSIONS QUALIFICATIONS?

Whereas previous metrics in the "Academic Qualifications" section deal with the reputation and quality of a school, the next set of metrics deal with the sub-heading "Admissions Qualifications."

› **Grade Point Average ("GPA")**

Grade point average is a calculation of the average grade you receive for classes taken. Calculations assign an "A" 4 points, a "B" 3 points, a "C" 2 points, a "D" 1 point, and no points for a failing grade. Some schools include pluses or minuses in the numerical assignment; for example, an "A-" earns 3.7 points, a "B+" 3.3 points, etc. Using this information determines an "unweighted" grade point average. Some schools also weight Advanced Placement and honors classes "with an extra point. Adding this detail determines a 'weighted' grade point average."[18] The grade point average is determined by adding up the points for all classes and dividing by the number of classes taken.

In the NACAC *State of College Admissions 2015* study, 91.3% of college admissions representatives believed that all grades were important to a college application for gaining admission.[19] It is equally important to make sure you are comparing apples to apples; for example, make sure your high school grade point calculation matches how the college will make the same determination. Some colleges do not include non-academic subjects (e.g., art, physical education, religion) in the calculation.

Others do not include pluses or minuses: a B is a B is a B, whether you earn a B+, a B, or a B-. Compare your unweighted high school GPA to the unweighted average GPA for admitted students to a college.

> ### High School Data

Some high schools subscribe to college preparation services (e.g., Naviance at *Naviance.com*) that track information for students admitted to a particular college or university *from your high school!* If your school does not offer such a service, ask your high school's college counselor for the following information:

- ○ **High School's Average Admit GPA (Score)** calculates the average unweighted GPA for students admitted to a college or university from your high school.

- ○ **High School's Average Admit SAT (Score)** calculates the average composite SAT score for students admitted to a college or university from your high school.

- ○ **High School's Low Admit SAT (Score)** represents the lowest composite SAT score for a student admitted to a college or university from your high school.

- ○ **High School's Average Admit ACT (Score)** calculates the average composite ACT score for students admitted to a college or university from your high school.

- ○ **High School's Low Admit ACT (Score)** represents the lowest composite ACT score for a student admitted to a college or university from your high school.

No two high schools are alike. Some are designated as "College Preparatory" with rigorous curricula. Likewise, some public high schools offer rigorous curricula, including several Advanced

Placement and honors course options. By compiling data specific to your high school, you will have a better gauge as to the kind of students a college may accept. Some colleges now assign admissions department officers to particular high schools within a region to compare student records within a high school and across the same schools year-over-year. Enter GPAs and standardized test scores for students from your high school accepted by a college into your research database under the corresponding heading.

› **National Data**

College Data.com, Peterson's Four-Year Colleges, Barron's Profiles of American Colleges, and *Fiske Guide to Colleges* collect the following metrics nationally:

○ **Average Admit Unweighted GPA** calculates the average unweighted grade point average for all admitted students to a particular college or university.

○ **Average Admit Weighted GPA** determines the average weighted grade point average for all admitted students to a particular college or university.

○ **Admit SAT Composite 25%-75% Percentile Score** represents the 25th percentile SAT composite score and 75th percentile SAT composite score for all admitted students to a particular college or university.

○ **Admit ACT Composite 25%-75% Percentile Score** shows the 25th percentile ACT composite score and 75th percentile ACT composite score for all admitted students to a particular college or university.

Enter the information into your research database under the corresponding heading. For test-optional schools, enter "Test Optional" for test scores.

WHAT ARE MY CHANCES OF GAINING ADMISSION?

High school specific and national data indicating the profile of students that apply to a particular school — and those that get in — will go a long way toward establishing the profiles of applicants and admitted students. A prospective student-athlete needs to compare the relevant statistics to his or her high school profile to determine the probability of getting in, and whether a college or university falls into the "reach," "likely," or "safety" category. Here are personal metrics to consider for "Admission Chances:"

› **Personal Data**

   ○ **Unweighted GPA**

   Calculate and enter your unweighted cumulative GPA from your latest high school transcript.

   ○ **Weighted GPA**

   Calculate and enter your weighted cumulative GPA from your latest high school transcript.

   ○ **SAT Composite Score**

   Enter your SAT composite score from your best exam. You may super-score results from multiple SAT tests, if the school considered accepts super-scoring.

   ○ **ACT Composite Score**

   Enter your ACT composite score from your best exam. You

may super-score results from multiple ACT tests, if the school considered accepts super-scoring.

Enter the information into your research database under the corresponding heading.

Also, several websites exist with which a student can enter GPA, test scores, and preferences about colleges in general, and the search tool produces a list of colleges and universities that match your profile. The websites most helpful for my recruiting process were College SuperMatch from Naviance, Big Future from the College Board, GPA and SAT or ACT graphs produced by Collegeapps.About.com, and academic profiles of admitted athletes on CollegeData.com "Admissions Tracker."

> **College SuperMatch, Naviance (Percentage)**

Naviance features a CollegeSuperMatch tool offered by many high schools and available through individual subscription. Users enter a series of criteria about their interests in college, including:

○ Location

○ Majors

○ My Scores

○ Tuition and Fees

○ Ethnicity

○ School Type

○ School Size

○ On-Campus Housing

○ Campus Setting

- Public or Private

- Gender Mix

- Historically Black

- Getting In

- Graduation Rate

- Organizations

- Special Services

- Disability Services

Not all criteria require an entry. Upon entering selected criteria, CollegeSuperMatch generates a list of colleges and universities along with the percentage to which each school matches user criteria, sorted from high to low. Enter the matching percentile for a school under consideration in your research database.

> **Big Future, College Board (Yes/No)**

Like Naviance's CollegeSuperMatch search engine, the College Board's Big Future allows users to enter criteria in search of colleges. Criteria include:

- "Test Scores & Selectivity," in which you can enter SAT or ACT scores and how selective admissions are for a school,

- "Type of School" (i.e., 2-year vs. 4-year, public vs. private, school size, co-ed vs. all women vs. all men, religious affiliation),

- "Location" (i.e., miles from home, by region or state, international), o "Campus & Housing" (i.e., setting, residential vs. commuter campus, on-campus housing guarantees, special living arrangements, cars permitted),

o "Majors & Learning Environment,"

o "Sports & Activities,"

o "Academic Credit,"

o "Paying,"

o "Support Services," and

o "Diversity"

Once a user enters preferences, the College Board produces a list of target schools that match criteria, segregating those with a "100% Match," meeting all of the criteria, from others meeting a portion or none of the criteria. The web page may be accessed at *bigfuture.collegeboard.org/college-search. Enter "Yes" ("Y") or "No" ("N") for whether a school under consideration gets listed by Big Future based on your profile.*

› **GPA and SAT or ACT Graphs, Collegeapps.About.com (Reach/Likely/Safety)**

Collegeapps.about.com produces a graph that plots unweighted high school GPAs and SAT or ACT scores among applicants to a college. Each dot represents one applicant. For similar grades and scores, graphs depict whether an applicant at that plot point was "Accepted" (green dot), "Accepted, Won't Attend" (blue dot), "Denied" (red dot), or "Waitlisted" (orange dot). The array for each respective college or university conveys the relative chances an applicant maintains to be accepted by the school. This tool provides an excellent way to discern which colleges represent a "reach," "likely," or "safety" based on whether your unweighted

GPA and SAT or ACT score lands you predominantly among red dots ("reach"), orange dots ("reach" or "likely") or blue and green dots ("safety"). The graphs may be found at *collegeapps.about.com/od/GPA-SAT-ACT-Graphs/*. Collegeapps.com was in the process of being acquired by ThoughtCo in 2017.

› **Admissions Tracker, CollegeData.com (Unweighted GPA, Weighted GPA, Test Scores)**

On CollegeData.com, users may enter a college or university to research its admissions history. A database exists for admissions by college graduating class dating as far back as 2010. Access the "College Admissions Tracker" portion of the website at *Collegedata.com/cs/admissions/admissions_tracker*. Submit the name of the school to be researched under "College Name" and select "Get Results." Numerous sorts exist by which to include multi-year statistics; the disposition of applicants (e.g., "Applied," "Accepted," "Denied," "Deferred," "Wait-Listed," "Not Applied," Withdrawn," "Pending/None" in any combination); "Decision Type" ("Regular," "EA/ED"); "Applicant Type" (e.g., "Standard," "Legacy," "Athlete"); gender; and high school location.[20] The website produces summary statistics for the school selected that include low/average/high unweighted and weighted GPA, SAT scores by test section, and composite ACT scores, including a graph. A prospective student-athlete may select "Athlete" to see how applicants in a similar situation fared. Enter the unweighted GPA, weighted GPA, and test scores for the school under consideration into your recruiting database.

So why compile other metrics when one of these websites can automate the process for you? First, you will want information in one place to reference as you navigate the recruiting process. Second, there are criteria that these website tools may not take into account. Third, sometimes the results for matching colleges do not reflect the raw data that exist on a college's website. While I do not recommend relying exclusively on these websites to identify schools to consider, they do provide feedback that can confirm or refute your research and evaluation of schools.

To be sure, there are other academic questions a prospective student-athlete should pose. Some of the questions may not be answered, however, until you have detailed conversations with a prospective coach or during official recruiting visits. Some of the academic questions include:

○ Does the school offer academic fields of study that interest me?

○ What is the level of academics? "Do the academic demands exceed my expectations? Are the academic demands not challenging enough?"[21]

○ What are the academic performance requirements to remain a student-athlete?

○ What emphasis does the coaching staff place on academics? What are the implications for a student-athlete (e.g., mandatory study halls, minimum grade point averages higher than NCAA minimum requirements, etc.)?

○ Does the school provide academic assistance? Is assistance provided to student-athletes or all students?

○ How do graduation rates among student-athletes compare to the graduation rate of the general student population?

Metrics may be added to your customized research database as appropriate.

› **Self-Assigned Summary (Reach/Likely/Safety)**

At the end of the "Academic Qualifications" portion of your research, it is a good idea to review the data amassed to identify potential schools of interest, compare your profile with other admitted students from your high school and nationally, and evaluate the results from college search website tools. Having compiled personal GPA and test score statistics, highlight the average GPAs and test scores for admittance to a college that are more favorable (i.e., lower) than your statistics in green, approximating your GPA and test score(s) in yellow, and less favorable (i.e., higher) than your GPA and test score(s) in red. Coloring can provide a visual reference for how your prospects may look for a particular school, if you are so inclined. From this information, you will be able to categorize colleges or universities in which you may be interested into "reach," "likely," and "safety" schools.

KEY SUMMARY POINTS:

Admissions Requirements

› Compare courses to meet high school graduation requirements with subjects for college admission early in your high school career to determine how to satisfy both sets of requirements.

› Compile information about application types, standardized tests, and recommendations accepted to meet expectations for college applications.

› Identify the application essays required and begin drafting responses over the summer between junior and senior year of high school.

Admissions Qualifications

› Compare your GPA and standardized test scores to those of accepted applicants at a college or university to determine your chances for admission.

› Classify colleges and universities being considered into "reach," "likely," and "safety" schools.

CHAPTER 4: **ATHLETIC QUALIFICATIONS**

The "Athletic Qualifications" section assesses the team in a particular sport at a school under consideration, and whether a coach may recruit you. Throughout this book, I do not presume to place academics over athletics or athletics over academics. The hallmark of a student-athlete involves opportunities and contributions in the classroom, athletic competitions, and the community.

Compiling helpful and accurate information about your athletic qualifications may be the most difficult task in your collegiate athletic recruiting process. Sure, you know how fast you run the 40-yard dash, how many unassisted and assisted tackles you made on the defense of your football team last year, or how many goals you scored on the pitch for your soccer team. But how do you climb into the mind of a prospective college coach to assess your qualifications? The best way is to ask him or her directly. Conducting some research by comparing the college team's level of performance and your athletic qualifications can inform the context around which to approach a coach.

Divided into "College Team Assessment" and "Personal Athletic Qualifications" sections, the following metrics may be added to your recruiting database and serve as a helpful starting point for assessing your "Athletic Qualifications" and how they compare to athletes on prospective college teams. Sources are listed as appropriate for each metric.

College Team Assessment

The "College Team Assessment" section includes general information and data to assess the number and ability of athletes on a college team:

›   **Current national rank, by division**

    This entry represents the national ranking for the college team under consideration in its respective sport and NCAA division. Enter the national ranking (#) or "NR" for not ranked.

›   **Division**

    Enter the corresponding division for the team and sport: Division I, Division II, or Division III, if applicable.

›   **Conference**

    In what conference does a school compete? The team's website states this fact. Teams for different sports from the same school do not necessarily compete in the same conference; for example, Stanford swimming competes in the Pac-12 Conference, while Stanford water polo competes in the Mountain Pacific Sports Federation Conference. Be sure to research in what conference the school competes for your particular sport. The conference can be an indication of the level of competition to expect.

›   **Number of roster athletes**

    How many athletes compete for the team? The team's website contains the number of athletes competing for the school under "Roster." The size of the roster can inform whether a coach accepts walk-ons (e.g., larger teams) or whether a coach directly focuses on elite athletes or does not maintain as large a budget (e.g., smaller teams). Comparing roster sizes of schools in the same conference particularly informs this insight. Count the number of players on the team. Enter the number into your recruiting database.

> **Number of graduating seniors before your entering class.**

While reviewing the roster, count the number of seniors that will graduate in the academic year before your incoming class. For example, if you are graduating high school in the spring of 2019, you will probably enter college in the fall of 2019. If you are accessing the website in the academic year 2017-18, then all of the juniors listed on the roster will graduate the year before you enter. Count up the number of team members that will graduate in the year before you enroll. This number represents a good proxy for how many recruits a coach may pursue in your class. Enter into your recruiting database the number of graduating seniors in the year before you would enroll.

> **Average recruits per year**

Staying on the team's webpage under "Roster," count the total number of the athletes on the team and divide by four. This calculation represents the average number of recruits a coach may pursue in any given year. The roster and year in school will uncover other insights as well. If there are differences in the number of athletes by class (e.g., six freshmen, two sophomores, six juniors, two seniors), then the coach may not be looking to "fill" a recruiting class but merely to take the best student-athletes available in any given year. If there is a decrease in the number of athletes by class (e.g., eight freshmen, six sophomores, four juniors, two seniors), you may wonder why athletes leave the program or whether there was a recent coaching change. Enter the average number of recruits by year into your recruiting database.

> **Voids to be filled by position**

Rosters on team websites may not only include the year in school but the position on the team or specialty events performed by an athlete. An example would be a catcher on the baseball team, a midfielder in lacrosse, or a freestyle sprinter on swimming relays. Identifying which positions graduating seniors vacate in the spring before you enroll, and determining whether there are underclassmen on the team to occupy vacated positions, will give some indication as to specific recruiting needs a coach may be looking to fill. Specify voids to be filled in your recruiting database.

> **Select top recruit profiles**

One of the best ways to understand the capabilities a coach looks to target in recruiting involves scouring the biographies of recruits that come before you. Some sports have specific recruiting websites that compile recruiting commitments by school. For example, *collegeswimming.com* maintains a recruiting page where a user can type in a school and find the list of signed recruits, including their rankings and competitive times. The other way to see profiles of recruits involves accessing the team page on the college website and going to "Roster." Many of the teams feature short biographies for their members. Click on the name of a freshman. Reference the paragraph for "Before [College]" or "High School." The athlete or coach typically provides information on international, national, state, and high school-level competitions, team captaincies, awards, and selected statistics. The other way to locate biographies is to search "News" and find an article about the team's most recent recruiting class. What better way to see whether your athletic qualifications match what a coach may be looking for than to compare yourself to the athletes he or she has already recruited? Make various entries in your recruiting database reflecting sample accomplishments of past recruits.

› **Recruiting standards, e.g., times (Yes/Unpublished/No/ Not Applicable)**

Some college programs require that a prospective student-athlete meet minimum requirements before he or she can fill out a recruiting questionnaire or be considered. The team page of the college website under "Prospective Recruits" often lists such standards. Look for links entitled "Recruiting Standards," "Minimum Times," or the like to see what minimum requirements may entail. If a school maintains standards and you meet them, this is your best indication of whether the coach may take an interest; however, it does not necessarily mean that you would be recruited. Enter "Yes" ("Y"), "Unpublished;" "No" ("N"); or "Not Applicable" ("NA"), based on the existence of recruiting standards.

Following "Academic Qualifications," the second part of the research database encompasses information about "Athletic Qualifications." Enter the information into your research database under the corresponding metric.

PERSONAL ATHLETIC QUALIFICATIONS

This section outlines your athletic qualifications compared to the expectations of a college team:

› **Recruiting standards met? (Yes/No/Not Applicable)**

If a college program requires recruiting standards, do you meet them? How close are you to achieving them? Indicate "Yes" ("Y"), "No" ("N"), or "Not Applicable" ("NA") for this field in your research database.

> **Stated recruiting expectations by coaches (Specify)**

After I expressed interest in a Mid-Atlantic research university's swimming team, an assistant coach replied, "To be considered as a recruit, you will have to maintain times that qualify for the A finals of our league championships in two events and the B finals of our league championships in one event." Pretty specific criteria. At first, I wondered if the fact that every swimmer on the team achieved equivalent times meant the school would not only win their league championships, but would do so in a dominating fashion. While I achieved times that qualified for last season's B finals at the league championships in three events, I did not meet minimum recruiting standards. While I was disappointed, her frankness in the recruiting process enabled me to avoid wasting precious time with that school. Enter specific recruiting standards and which ones you meet.

> **National rank (Ranking)**

List your national ranking in an individual sport or club/high school team ranking for a team sport, whichever is applicable.

> **State rank (Ranking)**

List your state ranking in an individual sport or club/high school team ranking for a team sport, whichever is applicable.

> **Awards and distinctions (Specify)**

List your awards and distinctions, including championships, captaincies, most valuable player awards, most inspirational awards, coaches' awards, and other athletic recognitions. Compare your credentials against those of signed recruits and athletes already on the team of a college or university.

> **Sample customized recruiting algorithm for your sport; e.g., swimming example**

Every sport is different. For swimming, I interviewed a former collegiate swimmer and three high school and club team coaches to get advice for how to objectively quantify whether I would be an attractive recruit to a prospective college coach. What they told me made a lot of sense. College coaches are there to win. Other than winning an NCAA championship, which only one team can win in each division (e.g., Division I, Division II, Division III) per sport each year, coaches want to win in their league. Therefore, the number of swimming events in which I would score points at the NCAA Championships or a given school's league championships represents the first measure in my customized recruiting algorithm. For swimming, the next level of winning occurs in dual meets. Results from these meets comprise a season record of wins and losses. With swimmers eligible to swim in only two individual events per meet plus relays — and with not every swimmer eligible to swim his or her best events — high school and club coaches suggested that I quantify the number of events where I would rank in the top three on a college team. This metric would indicate how likely I would be to score points for the team in dual meets. The last metric attempted to quantify the depth of my swimming across events. For colleges with small sports teams, a coach may need an athlete to be versatile, like a Swiss Army knife. In my freshman high school season, I swam competitively in nine different events! For a prospective college swim team, cumulative team rank in your top five events indicates quality, depth, and versatility. The following metrics are illustrative, specific to a customized recruiting algorithm for swimming:

○ **E.g., number of scoring events at NCAA or league championships.** Access the swimming results for the NCAA or school's league championships in the most recent year. Based on your times, see in how many events you would score for the team.

○ **E.g., number of events ranked in top three on team.** Compare your times to the times of members already on a given school's team in each event. Count up the number of events in which you rank in the top 3 for a specific team.

○ **E.g., cumulative rank on team in top five events.** Compare your times to the times of members already on a given school's team in your top five events. My top five events involved the 50 freestyle, 100 freestyle, 200 freestyle, 200 breaststroke, and 100 butterfly. If I ranked #3, #2, #4, #1, and #7 in these respective events, then my cumulative score would be the sum of those ranks or 17. Coaches I interviewed indicated that anything less than 20, or an average rank on the team of four in those events, would make me a potentially attractive recruit. The lower the cumulative score, the better.

I invite you to talk to coaches and develop a formula for evaluating the extent to which an athlete may get recruited in your sport.

SELF-ASSIGNED SUMMARY (RECRUIT/WATCH LIST/ NOT RECRUITED)

At the end of the "Athletic Qualifications" portion of your research, it is a good idea to review the data compiled to identify athletic teams of interest and compare your capabilities against those of other recruited athletes and team members. Among thousands of high school athletes in similar circumstances, it can be difficult to navigate peers that tell you "you're awesome," a well-meaning club and high school coach whose team's reputation will soar if colleges recruit his or her athletes, and veiled signals from college coaches. So how do you know when you are being recruited by a college coach? Based on my experience in talking to coaches and hearing stories from other prospective recruits on the recruiting trail, three classifications of recruitment exist: "Recruited," "Watch List," and "Not Recruited:"

›   **Recruited**

If a coach attends a prospective student-athlete's games, matches, or meets specifically to watch him or her perform, or if a prospective student-athlete gets called by a coach, asked to submit pre-read materials for admissions, or invited to participate in an official recruiting visit, he or she is probably being recruited. I had four different coaches call me at home to speak with me directly for a half-hour to an hour. Not all coaches may do this, but they wanted to evaluate my interest in the sport and their program. From my end of the conversation, they apparently wanted me to pursue their team. If a coach attends one of your competitions specifically to watch you compete, you are probably being recruited. Assistant coaches from two different colleges attended two different meets to watch me compete. Finally, coaches representing 17 colleges requested pre-read materials from me, and I submitted pre-read materials to 11 schools. 8 offered official recruiting visits, and I participated in four of them. Each of these steps represents signs that you are being recruited. Ultimately, what a coach says matters. If you hear, "You are a recruit. If you want to play for me next year, apply Early Decision; otherwise, there may not be a slot for you on the team," you are being recruited.

› **Watch List**

While better than not being recruited, but probably short of being recruited, a watch list is an in-between classification where a college coach demonstrates an interest in tracking your progress but does not fully commit to you as a recruit. The fact of the matter is, at an early stage in the recruiting cycle, a coach intends to see how the rest of a recruiting class may take shape and may not be willing to commit to anyone. In effect, a watch list means a coach has noticed you. A contact by a college coach to one of your coaches, or a personalized and ongoing dialogue with the coach via email all constitute examples of possibly being on a watch list. If a coach asks you to fill out a recruiting questionnaire on his or her team's website, you may get onto the watch list. While something sparked interest in reaching out to you in a generic fashion, he or she may simply be interested in compiling data about prospective recruits. The larger the database of prospective recruits, the better a coach may look in the eyes of an athletic director. Be sure to complete the recruiting questionnaire fully and accurately and to do so immediately. You are probably on a watch list if a college coach contacts your high school or club team coach. Three college coaches made calls to my club team coach to inquire about my ability and potential. I was so excited whenever this happened and wanted to hear from my club team coach exactly how each conversation went. While I was not being recruited yet, genuine interest existed. If a coach carries on an email dialogue with you over the course of time to "track your progress," you are not being recruited but remain on his or her radar.

› **Not Recruited**

Receiving brochures from colleges, getting invitations to sports camps, seeing coaches present at a competition, and filling out recruiting questionnaires do not constitute indications of prospective student-athlete recruitment. Receiving a glossy brochure from a college admissions office does not indicate recruitment of a prospective student-athlete at that school. Colleges circulate these brochures based on results from Preliminary Scholastic Aptitude Tests (PSATs) taken during the sophomore and junior years of high school. Direct-mail represents an example of push marketing; in this case, colleges try to get prospective students to apply. An invitation to a sports camp also does not reflect athletic recruitment. Sports camps on college campuses make money for the athletic department during off-seasons. While recruits may attend such camps, for most athletes, it is an opportunity to showcase skills. Unless a coach specifically indicates that he or she plans to watch you, a coach attending a game, match, or meet usually means he or she is there to recruit someone else. If you fill out a recruiting questionnaire on a team's website, you are initiating interest but that does not mean the coach will be recruiting you; you may not even get a response from the coach. A coach's response does not mean you are being recruited either; recruitment requires some other indication from a coach in the future.

KEY SUMMARY POINTS:

› Assess a college team to inform the composition of a team, the likely number of recruits desired, recruiting priorities and standards, and the profile of recent recruits.

› Compare your athletic qualifications to expectations, assess your contacts with coaches, and identify whether you would most likely be a recruit, on the watch list, or not recruited by the coach.

CHAPTER 5: **EXPECTATIONS AND FIT**

Expectations and fit involve a personal set of decisions expanding on the reflection completed in Chapter 1. Three categories of metrics inform an evaluation of fit: "School," "Program," and "Reputation."

SCHOOL

Several criteria assess the fit of a college or university under the heading "School," including:

› **Geography** represents the region of the country in which a college or university is located (e.g., "West," "Midwest," "Northeast," "Mid-Atlantic," "South").

› **Setting** describes whether the campus exists in a city (e.g., "urban"), in a populated area away from downtown (e.g., "suburban"), or in the country (e.g., "rural").

› **Size** can be determined in part based on undergraduate enrollment (i.e., number) or the campus footprint (e.g., "large," "medium," "small").

> **Type** encompasses several different trade-offs among school characteristics (e.g., "public" vs. "private," "co-ed" vs. "single-sex," "research university" vs. "liberal arts," "religion," etc.).

> **Affordability** does not represent the costs of tuition, fees, and room and board; rather, it shows how much the average student pays after scholarships and grants (i.e., average net price per year).

College guides, such as *Peterson's Four-Year Colleges, Barron's Profiles of American Colleges,* and *Fiske Guide to Colleges,* can be used to identify this information. Enter information compiled into your customized research database as appropriate.

PROGRAM

Other questions about expectations and fit a prospective student-athlete should pose involve the athletic program and team. Answers to some of the questions may not be understood until you conduct detailed conversations with a prospective coach or during official recruiting visits. Athletic-related questions about expectations and fit involve specific details about the program and team as follows:

> **How much practice time do coaches require per week?**

There may be no better way to evaluate your commitment to a sport than to understand what the time commitment will be for a particular program. The NCAA imposes practice limits by sport. Determine how many practices occur, the number of dryland or weight training sessions, and other commitments required of student-athletes on the team each week. Expectations for Division I athletes often exceed those for Division II and Division III athletes, but frequently those differences are negligible. To be a collegiate athlete, you are making a profound commitment to the sport at your school. Depicted is a sample email I received from a prospective coach about practice expectations:

From: [Coach]
Date: August 20, 2014 at 5:43:32 AM PDT
To: "Laura Dickinson '17"
Subject: Re: Recruiting: Laura Dickinson

Hi Laura,

Thanks for your interest in [College or University] - especially the swim program. These days we are balancing our time between organizing things for the upcoming season and enjoying a final few summertime adventures around [State]. It is a beautiful place - I hope you will get out here someday if you haven't. I know you are early in the process but it is never too soon to start gathering information. I am impressed with your progress and look forward to hearing more as you drop more time. You also swim for two amazing people so I have to guess you have a lot to offer in a team setting. For now, I will tell you some about the program and see what questions you might have.

There are roughly 45 men and women on the team from all over the country who meet each afternoon from 4:30 – 6:30 and mornings are offered as well. We begin our season on November 1st, swim 9 or 10 dual meets over the course of the next 16 weeks and end the season with a conference meet in February or Division III Nationals three weeks later. In January, we take a training trip – the whole team goes and it really brings everyone together as we head into the championship season. We don't have the longest season in the country but we manage to get the most out of it because we are extremely focused and enthusiastic.

We train to race rather than training to train. In the pool we have two priorities. First, we work to have excellent racing skills. We think things such as a thought out race plan, excellent sense of pace, effective pre-race warm up and post-race cool down are critical to success in the competitions. In order to race your fastest you also need to have great technique. We spend much of our aerobic time focused on the technique behind fast starts, turns, underwater swimming, breakouts and surface strokes – we use video every day. Obviously, a great race will be an all-out effort so we use demanding training sets in to challenge your choices because then the races will come naturally as you will have practiced all aspects many times in training.

Thank you again for the interest. Have a great year and keep in touch!

Sincerely,

[Coach]

Enter the "Practice Hours per Week" expected by a program into your research database.

○ **For co-ed sports, do men and women practice together or separately?**

For men's and women's teams that practice together, it can create an esprit-de-corps and relationships that grow your circle of friends on campus. It can also limit practice space and create distractions. In one case I researched, men's swimmers practiced at the main pool while women's swimmers practiced at an older, secondary pool. The environment in which you practice may profoundly impact your performance. While what you prefer remains your choice, become aware of how a college or university manages a co-ed sport. Enter "Yes" ("Y") or "No" ("N") depending on whether co-ed practices exist in the program.

○ **How adequate are the facilities?**

Endowments differ among colleges and universities, and schools invest in their athletic programs to different degrees and in dramatically different ways. Web searches and college visits represent the best way to discern differences among facilities.

To evaluate facilities before a visit, take a look at the athletics department website or team page for your sport at a given school. Many programs post a video tour of their facilities, narrated by a current student-athlete. Use a search engine, enter the college sports team, and view "Images" to see pictures of facilities and from competitions.

There is no substitute, however, for seeing the facilities yourself. During college visits, I witnessed varsity swimming pools that had not been re-plastered in years, the bottom of which looked like a map of Europe. I have seen college locker rooms that should have been shut down by the local health department long ago. On other visits, I experienced temples to the sport of swimming — gleaming facilities with world-class gym equipment, sparkling clear pool water, and amphitheater-style viewing areas. Under the heading "Facilities" in your research database, enter "Excellent," "Very Good," "Good," or "Poor."

○ **Do athletes room together? Do athletes eat together?**

One advantage of joining a college team is that it eases your transition to college. A college team affords a ready-made group of acquaintances sharing a common interest with whom you can acclimate yourself to new surroundings.

On the other hand, spending over twenty hours per week training and traveling on weekends to competitions may amount to plenty of time together. Investigate whether athletes on the team room together and eat together. Some coaches encourage shared housing but leave it up to the student-athletes. Frankly, if you awaken at 5:00 a.m. for morning practice, you may not be amenable to a night owl roommate who stays up until 3:00 a.m. I know of some prospective student-athletes on recruiting visits that made plans to sign-up for housing together. I prefer to room with another athlete, even if she is not from the same sport. At least we share many common expectations about our athletic commitments and schedules as student-athletes. Under the heading "Athlete Rooming" in the research database, enter "Yes" (i.e., "Y" when athlete rooming is required), "Optional" (i.e., athlete rooming is offered), or "No" (i.e., "N" when athlete rooming is not offered), accordingly.

The other consideration involving expectations and fit is whether athletes eat together. On some campuses, athletes eat among other athletes separately from the rest of the student body. On other campuses, athletes eat among the student body. The best way to research this information is to look at the college website under "Meal Plans." Some coaches also list this information on their team page. It may be important to investigate whether dining options remain available after evening practices. For "Athlete Dining" in the research database, enter "Yes" ("Y") or "No" ("N").

> **What are expectations during the off-season?**

While practice, head-to-head contests, and NCAA competitions or tournaments for most college sports encompass two-thirds of the academic year, in reality, athletics have become year-round endeavors. Seasonality will vary by sport and by coach. The NCAA may restrict the degree to which coaches conduct practices year-round, but many programs use team captain-led practices in the off-season. Be sure to ask about off-season expectations. Do athletes practice with their teammates? Are athletes expected to train with club teams in the area? It will be important to email a prospective coach with specific questions or to ask during official recruiting visits, as coaches rarely feature this kind of information on their team page. Enter "Yes" ("Y") for required off-season practices, "No" ("N") for no off-season requirements, "Captain-led" for off-season practices under a captain's direction, and "On-your-own" to meet expectations with a club-team or individually.

○ **How far does the team travel for competitions? What are professors' attitudes about making up work?**

One way to compile information about travel is to review the team schedule for the current season. Highlight away games, matches, or meets and identify where contests occur. For a local conference like the Southern California Interscholastic Athletic Conference (SCIAC) in the Greater Los Angeles area, all travel occurs by bus for up to a couple of hours from any one campus. For a regional conference like the New England Small College Athletic Conference (NESCAC), travel entails long bus rides or van pools through rural landscapes for several hours and some short plane rides. For a major conference like the Big Ten, schools are scattered across states from Iowa to Maryland requiring waits at airports and long plane rides. Confirming what you learn about travel from the team schedule involves emailing the coach. Under the "Travel" heading, enter "Planes," "Vans/Planes," or "Vans/ Busses" in your research database.

Ways to find out professors' attitudes about making up work involve emailing the coach, discussing it with prospective teammates on recruiting visits, and asking professors, advisors, or counselors who conduct information sessions as part of official recruiting visits.

○ **What rehabilitation programs are followed if you become injured?**

One way to test a program and athletic department's commitment to a student-athlete involves finding out how they manage an athlete's injury. While every case will be different, ask a trainer or conditioning coach on a recruiting visit what happens if you become injured. As Division I and Division II scholarships are only conferred one year at a time, it is possible a scholarship may be revoked at the end of the academic year in which a recruit becomes injured and cannot return to competition. Ask questions about potential scenarios. Enter "Yes" ("Y") or "No" ("N") in a "Rehab" column of your research database, depending upon whether a program follows an explicit rehabilitation program.

I found some coaches to be extremely willing to answer questions, as evidenced by the two-part email below:

Date: August 19, 2015 at 7:12:04 AM PDT
To: "Laura Dickinson '17"
Subject: Re: Update #5: Resumé and Questions

Hi Laura,

It is rare we meet such organized and thoughtful prospective students. I am really happy to know you liked what you saw at [College or University] and I will hope to keep the positive feelings going. You asked a number of great questions and we are knee deep in a number of projects these days. So I will likely take on a few of your questions at a time to have a better chance at sending you well thought out answers.

Team Goals and Culture

- *What are your goals for [College or University] women's swimming?* Each year we start talking goals in the fall but we actually put them to posters in our team room during our training camp once we have everyone back from abroad and have a sense of where people are. We always look to have what we call at least 100% improvement - that is everyone on the team improving by 1%, which is quite a stretch for a collegiate team. We try to choose team goals that we can control and judge our season through that. Of course we have a wish list of by products that keep us motivated: taking all five relays to nationals, finishing in the top 4 at conference or scoring over 1000 points at conference. All of those goals will happen if we swim as fast as I know we can so we just need to focus on times and to focus on times we need to train in the habits to swim those times.

- *How would you describe the culture of your team?* Positive, enthusiastic and dorky. I believe the swimmers love being part of the team because we strike a balance between focused hard work and light fun moments. We have women who strive to be All-Americans and women who want to score some points at the conference meet but they all have an equal chance to improve and they all contribute.

- *Are swimmers housed together?* Freshman year all athletes are separated from teammates to you will get to know a floor of people. Some of those people will be athletes on other teams and some won't be athletes. I hear many stories of swimmers who remain friends with the people they met on their floor freshman year I have to believe it is a great way to keep the campus from becoming divided between athletes and non-athletes. After freshman year everyone can choose who they live with and where they live - well, we have a lottery for it so they can choose where they would like to live but there is usually some compromise of course. Housing at [College or University] is amazing so there really aren't any bad options.

Recruiting Profile

- *What constitutes "recruitable" swim times?* I am attaching a pdf of our conference times. Our baseline goal for each recruiting class is two athletes who can final, two who can score in the top 16 and 2 who can at least score in the top 24. Our incoming class for this fall is better than average - 3 who can final, 3 who can finish in the top 16, one who can score in the top 24 in a couple of events and one we hope will return to form after a long illness. If she can do that she will score in the top 24 as well.

- *What represents the typical profile of swimmers admitted to [College or University] in terms of weighted GPA, unweighted GPA, and ACT?* Something like top 7% of the class. GPA is tough because so many schools so many different scales - lots of people have 4.3 or 4.4 out of 5.0. We see lots of people take 3 AP classes in Junior year and 3 more in senior. ACT scores are usually above 30 and we see a lot of 33/34. SAT's are usually in the high 600's for each section and we see a lot of 700's.

- *What is the lowest GPA required to still be considered as a recruit?* Tough one, maybe 3.3

What is the lowest ACT score required to still be considered as a recruit? Another tough one, maybe 25

OK, I will get back to you with more soon,

I hope your junior year is off to a good start,

[Coach]

Date: August 19, 2015 at 5:40:22 PM PDT
To: "Laura Dickinson '17"
Subject: Re: Update #5: Resumé and Questions

Hi Laura,

I am glad I am on the right track. A few more:

Recruiting Visits

- *How do you decide for whom to offer recruiting visits?* We typically invite in swimmers who can score in the top 16 and then add a few who have other things going for them like a sibling at the college or someone willing to apply without support and they have very strong academic credentials. I expect we will invite you to visit.

- *When would be the most appropriate time of year to make a recruiting visit?* If people are going for EDI we will set up a couple of weekends - probably one in late September and one in early October. This fall they are Sept 18-20 and Oct 2-4. After that we will use one more weekend for people who couldn't make either of those or are a little late to the process. If people are going Regular we will usually wait until after the decisions go out and we will then put together a weekend in mid to late April.

- *What does a recruiting visit involve and over what timeframe?* We usually set one up for Friday morning through Sunday morning. We will pick you up from the airport. Friday has an academic feel. Friday night we do some team activities. Saturday we go apple picking or to the beach. Saturday night is usually a walk into town or something fun on campus. Sunday we get you breakfast and bring you back to the airport. Californians have the option of coming in on Thursday night too. We do a lot of different things to make it all work when you are flying in from such a distance.

<u>Admissions</u> - As a general note. We have to be careful about the language we use surrounding admissions so some of these answers might be a little more vague. I can go into massive detail about our training or other things like that though!

- *Do you ever conduct "early reads" with admissions officers on behalf of recruits?* Yes

  - *What kind of feedback do you receive?* We have sort of a green light, yellow light, red light system for the pre-reads. It helps us know whether to keep going forward or not.

  - *Do you conduct early reads prior to visits?* Yes for the most part but it isn't required. I have 10 years of experience and can certainly tell when an outstanding candidate will make the cut. If they are also at the top of our impact list we might have them visit first and then do the read before applications are due.

  - *How consistent has that information been with admission results in the past?* Very consistent. We are a little more thorough in the process but I haven't had a surprise in all the years we have been doing things this way.

  - *Does Admissions send out "likely letters"?* This comes up a lot. No, we don't do likely letters. We do our best to communicate clearly and I can only promise I will be honest with you about your chances.

- *To what extent does the coaching staff have influence over the admissions decision?* If a candidate is 'supportable' all we need to do is decide who to support and things usually have a positive outcome. We typically admit a class of 7 or 8 women and I usually support 5 or 6 of those.

○ *Do you receive "slots" or "tips" for athletes?* Not exactly but a similar concept. More like an amount of support.

○ *Do you write a letter of recommendation on behalf of the recruit?* Yes and have follow up conversations with our liaison in admissions.

○ *How do you decide for whom to use slots, tips, or letters (e.g., top recruits vs. swimmers who may not get in on their own, etc.)?* I would say it is a little different each year. We look at our needs as a program, our needs down the road and how we can build the best class possible. Sometimes we will have to work a little with the whole department so we can matriculate the best class of athletes possible.

• *Do you require recruited swimmers to apply Early Decision?* No but we do acknowledge the 'bird in the hand' effect - that is if we can secure five or six solid women in EDI then I can focus on coaching for the season knowing we have a great group coming in. It also works well to know that when we offer support those candidates will come if they are admitted. I am sure you get that. I wouldn't say we require it but it seems things are moving that way more and more. We have a group of 8 women coming in this fall. Of that four were supported and five were admitted in EDI. One was supported and admitted for EDII and two more were admitted in Regular without support. That is a typical story for us.

○ *What are your stipulations around that process?* Not sure what you mean. We will verbally commit support and we expect you will apply. If we promise support and pull that support behind the scenes we will be in big trouble with admissions. We can't guarantee admission or anything but we will do what we can to convince you we will support you.

- ○ *If a recruit applies regular decision to all schools, would she still receive consideration as a recruit?* We will do our best. Here is my honest answer though. In the last five years we have held back support for the Regular round three times. Each time the swimmer went to another school. When that happens though we lose that support and don't have a chance to circle back with another choice. I have learned the hard way that it is probably better to do what we can for the ED rounds.

***All of that said, we are just getting to know our new president. The president has a huge influence over how all of these things work. In a year, we might be working with more support in the process and I might be working through things in a different way. I don't think we will be working with less support.

Candidacy

- At this point, how desired am I as a recruit to your swim team? Yes.

  - ○ *How many recruits do you have for the class of 2021?* Our database has around fifteen women with profiles in the ballpark of what we look for.

  - ○ *Where do I rank on that list?* I would say you are in the top five or six. We are always looking for strong freestylers, I have an affinity for

Californians and especially those from [Club Team] because I can only assume you bring more than just times to the table.

○ *Based on my profile, what degree of support would I potentially receive (e.g., slot, tip, letter)?* I can't answer that one yet but I believe you will be in that conversation.

OK, I hope that helps some. Feel free to bring on more.

[Coach]

REPUTATION

In addition to "School" and "Program," other considerations informing "Expectations and Fit" involve the "Reputation" for athletics and your particular sport.

› **How important a priority does the school place on athletics?**

Scour the website of a college to determine what emphasis it places on athletics generally, and what priority your sport draws. To gauge the prioritization of athletics, look at the school's main web page under "News." Review all of the news postings and see what proportion of articles deal with athletics. Does your sport ever make it onto the college's main news feed?

On some college websites, it's all about one sport. Others feature pictures of athletes and facilities for certain sports, but not others. To gauge the prioritization of your sport, look at the athletic department's main web page. What stories does it feature? Under "News," how many times does your team appear in an article? Gauge the "Athletic Priority" of sports at the school and enter "Low," "Medium," or "High" into your research database.

> **What is the reputation of this program?**

To gauge the reputation of a team, use a search engine and type in the particular college athletic team. In most cases, a few articles will surface about its accomplishments and potential problems. Many of the articles stem from the campus student newspaper or college website.

In my experience, I Googled an athletic team and found out the university suspended a program for hazing incoming freshmen on the team. As I was not particularly interested in being embarrassed before the first practice, I chose to drop that school from consideration.

While not part of initial research and evaluation, one of the best ways to understand the reputation of a program is from prospective teammates you meet during official recruiting visits and from other prospective recruits on those visits. Word gets around. Add comments (e.g., "Good program in weak conference," "Top 10 national program") about "Program Reputation" into your research database.

> **What is the reputation of the coaching staff?**

Similarly, a good way to research the reputation of a coach involves reading his or her biography and using a search engine to research and evaluate his or her impact on athletes.

When reviewing the biography on the team's webpage under "Coaching" or "Coaches," try to discern how accomplished the coach may be (e.g., NCAA championships, league championships, number of All-Americans), what other roles he or she may have (i.e., full-time coach, professor, other obligations), and for how long he or she has been at the institution and in coaching. If a coach maintains a track record of staying only four years at any one school, and he or she is in the fourth year of his or her tenure at the school you are considering, you may want to consider whether he or she will be there for the duration of your college career.

When I used a search engine to look up articles about a coach to provide insight, I discovered a glowing tribute to a long-standing coach and what made his student-athletes so successful in competition and the campus community. After reading the article, I wanted to compete for him!

One of the best ways to understand the reputation of a coach is from prospective teammates you meet during official recruiting visits, but those often do not take place until the beginning of your senior year of high school. Enter evaluative words like "Excellent," "Very Good," "Good," "Unknown," or other descriptive notes about "Coaching Reputation."

› **What is the level of athletic competition at the school? Within its league?**

Some student-athletes like winning; winning enhances the personality. They will pursue programs that are perennial winners of their leagues, if not NCAA championships. I know of one athlete whose sole criterion for picking a college was to land on the team that had won seven consecutive NCAA championships in her sport. If that's what is important to her, then she's making the right choice.

Some student-athletes like being a part of building something. This opportunity can entail rebuilding a winless program, resurrecting a program that was removed by the athletic department or banned by the NCAA, or starting a program from scratch. A Division II coach in the Midwest who was starting a new swimming program at his college approached me. While I did not pursue his interest, the opportunity to build something from the ground up intrigued me.

In assessing a program against your expectations, research

how competitive a team may be. For how long has the program existed? What was its won-loss record over the past five years? How did it perform in league championships over that period? Did it qualify for NCAA tournaments or championships? Enter "Low," "Medium," or "High" designations for "Level of Competition" in your research database.

○ **Have there been NCAA violations within the athletic department? Have they been imposed on the team in your sport?**

A search engine request should be able to answer these questions about the integrity of programs being considered using keywords "[College or University] NCAA Violations" and "[College or University] [Sport] NCAA Violations." If you learn of any infractions, enter your findings (e.g., "None," "Other Sports," or "Suspended by School") under "NCAA Violations — Athletic Department" or "NCAA/ School Violations — Program" headings.

Ultimately, the best way to assess expectations and fit is to visit a campus (see Section IV: Taking Campus Visits). Compiling a list of campuses to visit should be based on preliminary research outlined in these last three chapters. Cast a broad net. I recommend considering up to 20 to 30 schools at the outset of your recruiting process. Options will inevitably get scaled back based on your continued interest, a coach's continued interest, pre-read results, recruiting visit invitations, and offers (see Chapter 6, Scope of Outreach). You do not want to spend time visiting a school that you could already rule out based on research.

In the summer after my sophomore year, during the two weeks that I have off from year-round training, I visited 16 campuses along the Northeast and Mid-Atlantic corridor. I also visited four other campuses in Southern California on two different family vacations and two in the Midwest during a spring break. At nearly every campus, I participated in a student-led tour and attended an information session hosted by a representative from the admissions department. I did not choose to meet with coaches during these trips because I wanted to evaluate the college or university more broadly. Of the 16 campuses on the east coast, I ended up dropping eight from consideration just because they did not feel like a good fit for me. Every college campus gives off a vibe, and I felt fortunate to find eight in which I felt comfortable.

SELF-ASSIGNED SUMMARY (HIGH/MEDIUM/LOW)

At the end of the "Expectations and Fit" portion of your research, review the information to identify potential schools and programs that match what you seek. Categorize colleges or universities into "High," "Medium," or "Low" fit.

Regarding expectations and fit, a prospective student-athlete should ask two important questions:

1. Would I want to attend this college or university if I dropped the sport, got injured, or the school dropped the program?

2. Would I want to compete for this program if the coach left for another college?

KEY SUMMARY POINTS:

›   The scope of expectations and fit encompasses the characteristics of a college or university, expectations to compete on a team, and the program's reputation.

> › Compare the nature of the school and team with your expectations to identify whether the opportunity represents a "high," "medium," or "low" fit.

CHAPTER 6: **SCOPE OF OUTREACH**

How many programs should a recruit consider? How many should a recruit contact?

The size and scope of the endeavor depend on the results of the research performed and compiled in the chapters above. Research may show that there are dozens of programs or only a handful of programs in which you might be interested and where you can compete. Even with schools that appear to match your qualifications on paper, the scope of outreach should cast a broad enough net among schools to account for lack of interest on a coach's part, changes to your athletic capabilities or academic performance over time, changes to programs, and whether you will be accepted by a school.

While personal expectations and results will vary, I recommend the following scale to help define the scope of outreach by a recruit:

Outreach Scale Ratios

> 20-24 recruit-initiated contacts to coaches

> 12-16 courtesy replies

> 8-12 pre-reads requested

> 4-6 recruiting visit invitations

> 2-4 official visits taken

> 2 offers conferred

> 1 offer of admission accepted

Indeed, this scale can be geometrically increased depending on the interest from coaches and your appetite for fielding requests from coaches. I am aware of national-level high school athletes who receive over 100 expressions of interest from coaches. Other recruiting services recommend a minimum of 50 contacts. The key is to keep a broad enough set of options open because your preferences will change throughout the process and "stuff happens" along the way.

Not all recruit-initiated contacts to coaches will receive a reply. A coach may not actively be recruiting for athletes in your class until a year before high school graduation. A coach may look at your credentials, not be interested, and not extend the courtesy of a reply. Even if a coach is interested, coaches maintain depth charts of recruited athletes, and the odds are overwhelming for any one recruit to be offered a spot on the team. For these reasons, I recommend initiating contacts with more schools than you expect from which to receive replies. Of the 24 recruit-initiated contacts I made, only 16 coaches replied.

Among the courtesy replies, Division I coaches may indicate

that they will not pursue student-athletes until after their junior year of high school, per NCAA regulations. Other coaches invite the correspondence but recognize at an early stage of the process that other prospective recruits will come along as well.

After corresponding with a prospective student-athlete for an extended period, a coach may lose interest in a recruit; alternately, the recruit may lose interest in joining the program or attending the school. A recruit's grades and test scores may not be sufficient for a coach to extend a pre-read to determine whether to invite the recruit for an official recruiting visit (see Chapter 18, Pre-Reads). For these reasons, I recommend maintaining consistent contact with more coaches than you expect to ultimately be more closely evaluated by toward the end of the recruiting process.

While a coach may request an academic transcript, standardized test scores, and other pertinent information to help an admissions officer evaluate your admissions potential, you still may not receive a "green light" and therefore an official recruiting visit invitation (see Chapter 19, Official Recruiting Visits). Even if your chances remain decent for gaining admission, it is at this point in the recruiting process when a coach can weigh one recruit's profile against another. A coach only offers a limited number of weekends on which to host prospective student-athletes for official recruiting visits. Every program that invited me for an official recruiting visit offered at least two recruiting weekends during the fall of senior year in high school. One Division I school on the east coast offered a choice among five weekends. Always attempt to participate in more pre-reads than official visits anticipated because not all programs will extend an official visit invitation and some invitations may conflict with each other.

Exceptions to these ratios exist. For the blue-chip recruit that can probably land with any Division I team, he or she may simply hand-pick a few programs to pursue. Such a recruit probably didn't have to pick up this book. One nationally-ranked swimmer on my club team only selected three schools on which to go on official recruiting visits and did not prolong the recruiting process leading up to those visits.

For most prospective student-athletes looking to conduct an intentional recruiting process, I recommend selecting up to two dozen schools to target in a push marketing campaign (see Chapter 9, Push Marketing). You can always end correspondence with a coach downstream, but it becomes extremely tough to initiate a relationship with a coach late in the recruiting process.

High school counselors recommend including approximately one-third "reach" schools, one-third "likely" schools, and one-third "safety" schools among targets. In athletic recruiting, a "reach" school could represent a swim team that would be difficult to be recruited for or make, or a school where it would be difficult to gain admission academically. A "likely" school involves a college where you are likely to make the athletic team and likely to gain admission. "Safety" schools involve programs where a recruit would contribute significantly to the athletic team and assuredly gain admission.

Consistent with my research results and the scope of outreach in this chapter, I sent emails to 24 NCAA programs beginning in the summer after my freshman year. I selected the schools where I could possibly get in, contribute to the swim team, and would be interested in enrolling. Throughout the course of my recruiting process, I ended up adding four more programs to my push marketing campaign (see Chapter 9, Push Marketing): three that contacted me through pull marketing (see Chapter 8, Pull Marketing) and one that I added myself. You can always add or drop programs and coaches from your target list.

KEY SUMMARY POINTS:

› While the circumstances and experiences of each recruit will vary, the scope of outreach to coaches at schools should be broader than you might expect.

› For every one offer of admission accepted, I recommend reaching out to up to two-dozen programs.

› "Stuff happens" (e.g., coaches do not reply, coaches lose interest, pre-reads get rejected, official visits do not go well, recruits lose interest) throughout the recruiting process.

› Your list of colleges and universities being considered will fluctuate over time based on contacts from coaches at programs not previously considered and new options you discover.

CHAPTER 7: **SELECTION OF SCHOOLS TO PURSUE**

Which programs should you contact?

If there are more colleges and universities than can be reasonably managed, it helps to prioritize options before making initial contact. I did this evaluation by making a 2x2 chart of possible schools and programs.

College Prioritization
2x2 Matrix

High	**High College / Low Team** School E School G School L School N School O	**High College / High Team** School A School D School I School J School K School M School F
College "Fit"		
	Low College / Low Team School H	**Low College / High Team** School B School C School F
Low		
	Low **Team "Fit"** **High**	

The vertical axis represents college fit. Criteria that comprise this axis include academic fit (e.g., do my grades and test scores fall within the range of applying students? admitted students?) and other academic considerations. High and low designations are used to assess each school's relative academic fit. The horizontal axis represents team fit (e.g., will I likely be recruited? can I make contributions to the team? is the school committed to my sport? is it a reliable program?). In this way, the "Athletic Qualifications" dimension gets incorporated with "Expectations and Fit" considerations. Again, high and low designations are used to assess the team in your sport at a given school.

Those schools emerging in the upper-right-hand "High College-High Team" box demonstrate a strong academic and athletic team fit. These names moved to the top of my list. Those schools emerging in the lower-left-hand "Low College-Low Team" box show a poorer fit. A school in the "High College-Low Team" quadrant exhibits a better college fit but a poorer team fit. Likewise, a school in the "Low College-High Team" quadrant represents a poorer college fit but a better team fit.

While you should consider each school on a case-by-case basis, a recruit should also ask to what extent he or she weighs college fit over team fit? In my estimation, you never know whether a coach will leave a college program, a school will drop an athletic team, or you will become injured. In these circumstances, I believe you have to be comfortable at the school you choose more so than the sport. As such, I weighted "High College-Low Team" schools slightly ahead of "Low College-High Team" schools.

There exists a fair amount of subjectivity in this exercise, but if you have performed the detailed research described above, you will have a good sense as to the quadrant in which a school/program gets placed. If you are looking for a more objective approach, you can always select one quantifiable metric to use on each axis. For example, at one point in evaluating programs to target, I used the most recent *Forbes* college rankings, which unlike *U.S. News and World Report*, combine national universities and liberal arts colleges into one poll. For the vertical axis, I used the best rankings at the top of the axis. On the horizontal axis, I used the NCAA team ranking with the best rankings to the right of the horizontal axis. You can choose whatever criteria are most important to you to array programs. Again, the most important aspect of this exercise is to identify a broad basket of options to initially contact, a collection that may change over time.

KEY SUMMARY POINTS:

> The number of programs to contact will depend on the research conducted (e.g., Academic Qualifications, Athletic Qualifications, Expectations and Fit), and how well you can reasonably manage communications at one time to and from multiple schools.

> A 2 x 2 matrix can be used to prioritize schools and teams.

SECTION III MARKETING YOURSELF

CHAPTER 8: **PULL MARKETING**

"Don't bother with recruiting. Improve your performances and the phone will ring."

This statement rings true for many blue-chip athletes in their sports. A household name known by every NCAA Division I coach around the country makes that athlete's phone ring. For the vast majority of high-school athletes, however, the phone will never ring without self-promotion.

Promoting yourself is intentional and necessary in college recruiting. For most prospective student-athletes, I recommend beginning as early as the end of your freshman year of high school, if not earlier, and no later than the end of your sophomore year of high school.

As in corporate marketing, promotional strategies to get you, your academic qualifications, and your athletic credentials in front of college coaches involve two different techniques: pull marketing and push marketing.

Push marketing entails taking your credentials directly to a coach (i.e., taking the product to the customer), detailing your commitment to the sport, expressing your interest in a particular college or university, and outlining your academic and athletic credentials.

Whereas Chapter 9 deals with push marketing tactics and examples, the remainder of this chapter delves into pull marketing.

Pull marketing attempts to motivate coaches to seek you out (i.e., getting the customer to come to you). Examples of pull tactics involve profiles filled out on recruiting websites, (e.g., NCSA Recruiting or CaptainU for athletes in any sport and CollegeSwimming.com for swimmers), mass media promotions (e.g., posting videos on YouTube), and word-of-mouth referrals.

› **Sport-specific vs. general recruiting websites**

Athletic recruiting websites involve two types: sport-specific and general recruiting websites. A sport-specific website is dedicated to one sport and often compiles competitive results on athletes. A website for general recruiting accommodates recruits from many sports. When filling out a profile, the general websites request the sport(s) in which you are interested in being recruited and sort recruits by sport. The broad nature of these websites, however, may make them less focused for recruits and coaches in a given sport.

An alphabetized list of websites for general athletic recruiting follows:[22]

General Athletic Recruiting Websites

Website Name	Web Address
ABC Athletic Recruiting	*abcathleticrecruiting.com*
Athlete Recruiting Services	*athleterecruitingservices.com*
Athletes for College	*athletesforcollege.com*
Athletic Aid	*athleticaid.com*
Athletic Quest	*athleticquest.net*

Athnet Sports Recruiting	*athleticscholarships.net*
Go Big Recruiting	*gobigrecruiting.com*
Ivy Recruiting	*ivyrecruiting.com*
National Scouting Report	*nsr-inc.com*
NCSA	*ncsasports.org*
Premier Athletic Recruiting	*premierathleticrecruiting.com*
Recruit Look	*recruitlook.com*
Recruiting Realities	*recruitingrealities.com*
USAthletic Recruiting	*usathleticrecruiting.com*
Varsity Edge	*varsityedge.com*

> **Fee-based vs. free websites**

Some athletic recruiting websites are fee-based while others are free. Fees can be one-time payments or annual subscriptions. You will have to decide on a case-by-case basis whether the information compiled and services offered warrant paying for them.

> **Information requested**

Information requested by recruiting websites often involves background information, contact information, academic information, athletic results, and photos or videos. As an example, the CollegeSwimming.com website requests:

○ "Basic Information," including name, nickname, gender, date of birth, height, and weight.

○ For "Contact Information," the website requests country, street address, city, state, zip code, home phone number, and mobile phone number. It also asks how often you would like to be contacted by coaches and by what medium (e.g., email, phone, text).

○ Under the "Academic" portion of the profile, the website asks for high school graduation year, college enrollment year, intended major, ACT scores, SAT scores, unweighted GPA, NCAA Eligibility Center number (see Chapter 10, NCAA Eligibility Center), and academic honors and awards.

○ "Athletic" results for this website compile times from sanctioned USA Swimming meets.

○ The "Photos and Videos" portion of a recruit's profile offers the opportunity to upload a portrait and videos that give coaches an image of your athletic ability.

Most recruiting websites maintain a database of athletes' profiles, compile a database of interests for each program, and link the two — offering coaches a customized list of athletes in which they might be interested. Thus, it is important to include as much information as possible so that coaches can match your qualifications to their level of interest.

› **Stipulations from coaches**

One coach from a Midwestern college requested that I sign-up for a particular recruiting website, CaptainU, that he uses to track recruits. No other coach made such a request, but I had no problem complying. As a result, you may be managing different marketing strategies and websites, depending on the schools that express an interest in you or the schools in which you maintain an interest.

> **Updates**

Some websites, like CaptainU, provide updates anytime a coach accesses your profile.

Updates include the number of coaches accessing your profile,

From: " CaptainU" <help@captainu.com>
Date: December 17, 2015 at 4:30:35 PM PST
To: "Laura Dickinson"
Subject: You were found 27 times by swimming coaches!
Reply-To: help@captainu.com

Hi Laura – way to go! This year, you were found 27 times on CaptainU by swimming coaches!

– Eric @ CaptainU

A coach reviewing your profile,

From: CaptainU <help@captainu.com>
Date: September 29, 2015 at 11:24:46 AM PDT
To"Laura Dickinson"
Subject: This coach checked your profile...

Great job, Laura –

A college coach just looked at your profile on CaptainU!

A coach indicating that your profile matches their interest,

From: CaptainU <help@captainu.com>
Date: April 11, 2016 at 12:38:06 PM PDT
To: "Laura Dickinson"
Subject: You're a match!

Hi Laura – Good news! A college coach ran a search on CaptainU, and your profile is a match!

Congratulations! Keep it up!

Or a coach wanting to make contact with you,

From: CaptainU <help@captainu.com>
Date: September 8, 2015 at 1:47:01 PM PDT
To: "Laura Dickinson"
Subject: A coach messaged you!

Congrats, Laura – a coach sent you a message on CaptainU!

Athletes who reply to a coach are much more likely to make the team!

Good job!

–The CaptainU Team

› **Identification of target schools**

Based on the response you may get from pull marketing efforts, if any, an athlete will be able to gauge the kind of schools that want to target him or her. Even if you are not interested in one of the coaches that accesses and acts on your profile, it still gives you a sense of target schools. For example, if a coach from a top ten Division I university in your sport makes contact, then you might surmise that other top-ranked programs may be interested as well. If a coach reaches out to you from a small liberal arts college where admission remains extremely tough, you might conclude that you have the academic credentials and athletic hook to get into similarly-regarded schools. However, a school not contacting you doesn't necessarily mean they are not interested; they may just not have initiated recruiting for your class.

> **Comparisons to other athletes**

On sport-specific websites that compile competitive results, athletes will be able to compare where they rank athletically against other prospective recruits. For example, CollegeSwimming.com groups recruits by gender and high school graduation class. Athletes receive a dashboard listing a power index using a percentile ranking, a state ranking, and a national ranking based on their two best events.

> **Exposure**

Probably the greatest impact of pull marketing remains the broad exposure it confers in a few easy steps. The Next College Student Athlete (NCSA) website purports to give exposure for athletes to over 42,000 college coaches.

I completed two recruiting profiles, one general website where you indicate your individual sport (e.g., CaptainU) and one website specific to my sport (e.g., CollegeSwimming.com). Neither of these websites charged a fee for doing so. If your sport maintains a recruiting database, I highly recommend that this be something in which you participate at a minimum. Also, I completed the NCAA Eligibility Center steps discussed in Chapter 10, NCAA Eligibility Center.

I avoided other fee-based services. In my subsequent conversations with coaches, I learned that assistant coaches and graduate assistants scour the recruiting services and websites to compile prospective student-athlete targets. I also realized, in hindsight, that if you pursue a rigorous push marketing strategy as described in Chapter 9, entitled Push Marketing, you should not have to pay someone to market your services.

In my recruiting experience, coaches and assistant coaches from schools for which I was athletically qualified to swim for their programs contacted me with emails to solicit my interest based on these pull marketing website profiles. In the emails they indicated that they had viewed my profile.

From: [Coach]
Date: May 20, 2016 at 2:58:25 PM PDT
To: "Laura Dickinson"
Subject: Just what you were looking for...

Hi Laura,

Can you get back to me today on this? I really want to talk with you!

I'm getting in touch because I've seen your profile, saw your times, and I'm pretty sure I want you to swim for me here at [College or University] after your high school career is done.

I wanted to get that out of the way right at the beginning, so you would know exactly where you stand with us. I also want to learn more about you, tell you more about us, and figure out if we might be a good consideration.

Just to start things off, Laura, I wanted to ask you three questions:

- Do you want to swim for a program where you're a priority and can compete at a conference - and maybe even *national* - level starting your first year in college?

- Do you want to graduate with one of the best, affordable

educations in the Northeast, at one of the "Best Value Colleges" in the country?

I'm hoping your answer is "yes", Laura, because that's what I'm offering you. Can we talk more about it?

To get things started, I need two things from you right away (at least before this next weekend):

1. If you have real interest please fill out our Recruit Questionnaire. It'll only take a few minutes, and it will really help me get to know you.

2. Get in touch with me. I really want to talk to you for a minute or two: Just reply back or give me a call...I want to know that you got this, and ask you two or three questions.

Sound good, Laura? Let's talk...I hope to hear from you soon!

Thank you,

Best Regards,

[Coach]

In total, 29 programs contacted me based on profiles I set up on recruiting websites. Of these, four were Division I, four were Division II, and 21 were Division III programs. None of them comprised my original list of target schools, but I was pleased to receive their communications, learn about some institutions with which I was not familiar, and pique my interest in three of them that remained on my target list throughout the collegiate athletic recruiting process.

Pull marketing efforts will help athletic recruits with exposure, identification of target schools, and an evaluation of your athletic credentials. Pull marketing matters, and also mutually reinforces the push marketing contacts you make to schools in which you are interested.

KEY SUMMARY POINTS:

› There are two main types of marketing to increase your exposure as a prospective student-athlete: pull marketing and push marketing.

› Pull marketing involves posting your academic and athletic credentials on recruiting websites, on sport-specific websites, and in mass media promotions (e.g., YouTube, personal web pages).

› The information you provide will help a broad number of coaches evaluate you among other recruits; the responses you receive will help identify potential target schools.

CHAPTER 9: **PUSH MARKETING**

For the vast majority of high school athletes, the phone will never ring without self-marketing. As already stated, promoting yourself is intentional and necessary in college recruiting. Pull marketing represents the first step in getting your qualifications "out there" to a broad and unspecified range of coaches. Push marketing entails presenting your credentials directly to a coach (i.e., taking the product — "you" — to the customer) through correspondence.

Prospects initiate an interest in a specific program, encouraging the coach to recruit him or her. Developing a push marketing campaign will demonstrate initiative, confidence, and other qualities for which a coach may be looking. To begin a push marketing campaign, you will need to decide: whom to contact, what information to provide, when to make initial contact, and how often to make contact.

› **Whom to contact?**

One of the most important things to do before sending out correspondence is to research whom to contact and how they prefer to receive communication. Consult the team page of the school's athletic website under "Contact Us" or "Coaches" to discover email addresses, phone numbers, addresses, and other contact information. In a couple of instances, I visited the school's main website and consulted the "Faculty and Staff Directory" to find contact information for a coach. Be resourceful. You are better off sending correspondence directly to a coach instead of using the general contact information for the athletic department.

A team may have a head coach and one or more assistant coaches. In some instances, an assistant coach may be in charge of recruiting. For an initial introduction, I sent an email to the head coach with carbon copies to the assistant coach(es). Copying down the correct contact information and adding it to your contact database (see Chapter 14, Contact Database) for future reference is imperative! If you send information to the wrong place or email address, the coach may never receive it and you will conclude that he or she does not have an interest in you. Also, spelling names of coaches and schools correctly will demonstrate your attention to detail.

> **What information to provide?**

To reinforce communications with coaches and strengthen college applications, prospective student-athletes should track extracurricular and athletic activities, achievements, and awards. To remember and prioritize what you accomplish in high school, I recommend keeping a log and establishing headings for "Academic," "Athletic," "Arts," "Community," and "Leadership." While activities and honors before high school can be considered, the Common and Coalition Applications ask that the high school grade level (i.e., 9-12) be specified for each activity and honor. Once you have compiled a list of accomplishments, reflect on the story they tell about you; that is, how do entries collectively distinguish you as a recruit and college applicant?

The initial contact with a coach involves making an introduction. Provide enough information to give the coach a sense of your interest in his or her program and reasons why he or she should put you on the radar. Content can include: name, high school, year in high school, interest in college, GPA, courses, awards and honors, training schedule, key statistics, upcoming competitions, and contact information. I recommend keeping each correspondence to one page. Depicted is the introductory email I sent to targeted programs:

RE: Recruiting Introduction

Dear Coach XXX,

My name is Laura Dickinson, and I begin my sophomore year this fall at [High School] in [City]. After graduating in 2017, I am interested in attending [College or University]and participating on the women's swimming team because of College or University] dedication and balance among academics, service, and athletics that will allow me to excel in each area.

With a weighted GPA of XX, including AP and Honors classes in Algebra and French freshman year, and Geometry, French, Spanish, and English sophomore year, I believe I stand an excellent chance of getting into College or University]. As a freshman, I earned National French Honor Society, California Scholarship Federation, California Interscholastic Federation (CIF)/Central Coast Section (CCS) Scholar Athlete, and Principal's Honor Roll achievements.

Before committing two years ago exclusively to competitive swimming year-round, I was a five-sport athlete in swimming, water polo, basketball, tennis, and volleyball, achieving 26 team and individual championships in 17 seasons. I currently participate in dry land training daily with [Name of Facility] fitness and swim ,

18-20 hours weekly with coaches [Coach 1] and [Coach 2] at [Club Team].

Laura Dickinson Best Times Progression	Age	Time	Difference
50 Y Free	13	28.03	
	14	26.24	-1.79
	15	25.37	-0.87
100 Y Free	13	1:02.31	
	14	58.77	-3.54
	15	55.05	-3.72
200 Y Free	14	2:18.15	
	15	2:00.62	-17.53
50 Y Breast	13	34.03	
	15	32.27	-1.76
100 Y Breast	13	1:21.04	
	14	1:15.25	-5.79
	15	1:12.21	-3.04
200 Y Breast	13	3:00.26	
	14	2:42.52	-17.74
	15	2:34.41	-8.11
50 Y Fly	13	28.45	
	14	27.40	-1.05
	15	27.19	-0.21
100 Y Fly	13	1:11.72	
	14	1:05.12	-6.60
	15	1:00.05	-5.07

Capable of competing in and contributing to several strokes and relays, I qualified in eight events for the California CCS meet my first high school season. I am a California CCS finalist, three-time Pacific Swimming Zone champion, five-time high-point swimmer, 12-time swim league champion, and 31-time USA Swimming medalist. The progressions in the table provided reflect not only my starting to swim at age 10, but also pursuing opportunities for continued improvements based on my exclusive commitment to full-time swimming.

Please consider this email to be an introduction, and I look forward to keeping you apprised of my progress.

Sincerely,

Laura Dickinson

If you are using the same correspondence for multiple programs, be sure to customize fields for the coach's name, school name, address, etc.

In your ongoing updates, it's always a good idea to include academic, athletic, and community information as appropriate — things that highlight the dimensions of a student-athlete. Depicted is a sample update I sent quarterly to targeted programs and a coach's response:

On Wed, Mar 2, 2016 at 5:06 PM, Laura Dickinson

Dear [Coach],

Congratulations on [College] women's swimming and diving team's performance at the [Name] Conference Championships last month! Thank you for keeping me apprised of your team's activities and accomplishments.

I wanted to update you on my academic and swimming progress. Last semester at [High School] in [City], I earned a XX weighted GPA, taking English Honors, Spanish 3 Honors, PreCalculus Honors and AP U.S. History as accelerated and advanced courses. My combined cumulative high school GPA is now XX weighted (XX unweighted). I also took an AP [Subject] test scoring XX and the [Subject] SAT II subject test scoring a XX. My plan is to take two additional SAT II subject tests this spring, and the ACT in April and again in June, if necessary.

In the pool, I have been working on freestyle sprints. In my four years of swimming on a USA club team, with North Bay Aquatics, this is the first time I've focused on a particular stroke and distances. At the UC Santa Cruz meet last month, I swam in three A finals logging a :24.66 best time in the 50 free, :53.44 in the 100 free, and 1:57.03 best time in the 200 free. At the [Name] meet in Clovis last week, I swam a :24.81, :24.66, :24.45, and then a :24.29 in the 50 free finals under the lights. With this best time, I qualified for NCSA Junior Nationals in Orlando later this month and the USA Swimming Futures Championships this summer. I am now turning my attention to our spring high school season, having been named team co-captain as a junior.

I hope you will continue to consider my qualifications as the recruiting season ramps up.

Sincerely,

Laura Dickinson

[High School]

Class of 2017

Top times:

50 free	:24.29
100 free	:53.20
200 free	1:57.03
200 breast	2:26.38

From: [Coach]
Date: March 3, 2016 at 10:28:00 AM PST
To: Laura Dickinson
Subject: Re: Update #7

Hi Laura,

Thanks very much. We did have another strong end to our season this year and are fired up to take a great group to Nationals in a couple of weeks.

It looks like you are swimming fast and I am sure you will have some inspired swims for your HS team this spring. Keep up all the great work and I look forward to talking more specifically about college once you finish up your junior year.

Take care,

[Coach]

In each instance, I would only send information that showed meaningful progress; for example, grades from my latest term, a new class schedule, improved times, and new awards.

> **When to make initial contact?**

NCAA rules prohibit Division I or Division II coaches from responding to a recruit until September 1 at the beginning of their junior year or contacting recruits before June 1 following their junior year of high school. For one Division I program, the coach indicated as much in his correspondence with me:

From: [Coach]
Date: August 20, 2014 at 8:00:45 AM PDT
To: "Laura Dicksinson"
Subject: Dickinson, Laura '21

Please note that due to NCAA guidelines I cannot respond to your email until September 1 at the beginning of your Junior year. If you are interested in the [College or University] Swimming program, below is a link to our questionnaire:

Thank you.

A Division I or II coach may not contact a recruit until the recruiting period opens. If this is the case, how can high-profile recruits receive verbal offers from colleges and universities well before that point in time? A recruit is allowed to contact coaches as much as he or she wants (see Chapter 15, NCAA Recruiting Guidelines and Rules). For most athletes, I recommend beginning as early as the end of freshman year of high school – if not earlier – and as late as the end of your sophomore year of high school.

› **How often to make contact?**

The frequency of push marketing contacts depends on the recruit. Some recruits only respond to coaches that initiate a contact after the first correspondence. Other recruits communicate quarterly, monthly, or even send weekly tweets. You may call or email a coach as often as you would like, but to be respectful, I recommend doing so when you have new pertinent information to influence your recruiting profile. I chose to send quarterly updates to coaches; that way, I could provide new information, maintain interest, and not overwhelm my other responsibilities in high school. The other factor determining frequency of contacts involves detecting the interest a coach may have in you as a recruit based on the pattern of communication from the same coach and program over time.

Before sending correspondence, it is imperative to customize and proof-read your communication… every last word! Check for spelling, grammar, and editing errors. Do not simply rely on a word processing program to check for mistakes. *Read* your correspondence before sending it. There are instances, as when you send an update about your academic, athletic, and community progress, where you primarily use the same text for multiple schools. Be very careful! Nothing will turn a coach off more than if you mention another school to which you sent your last correspondence because you failed to change the name of the school, other school-specific detail, or coach's name.

After sending emails, it is also imperative to maintain a contact database, the design and use of which Chapter 14 discusses. You will not be able to remember every contact you make with multiple coaches over the course of a two or three-year period. You will also want to update any information about changes to a college's coaching staff since your first contact. The contact database helps keep track of every contact you make with coaches and their replies. I ended up consulting the database on multiple occasions to answer: whom to contact, what have I already sent them, what did the last conversation entail, and who's really interested.

Evaluating coaches' responses remains as important as what you send in a push marketing campaign. While you will want to avoid reading into every communication you receive literally, feedback will provide context and clues about the individual programs and the interest shown by coaches, as follows:

›   **Responsiveness**

Whether and how quickly a coach responds to your correspondence can provide valuable insight. If a coach does not return a phone call or respond to written communication, check to make sure you used accurate contact information. No response after an extended period probably means the coach is not interested in you as a recruit, not recruiting your class at that time, or not on top of things. I had one coach who answered instantaneously but was not interested — the sign of a responsive and honest coach. I received replies from a couple of coaches who said that they would keep my correspondence and refer to it in the spring of my junior year when they would begin recruiting my class — the sign of honest coaches that may or may not have significant program resources. Due to a coach's vacation and other commitments, I would give a coach a couple of weeks to reply before moving a program down or off my target list. Some simply do not respond or stop responding. At the beginning of my recruiting effort, I hung on every incoming email to see if a coach responded to my communication. As time went by, I checked recruiting correspondence once or twice a day.

> **Customization of messages**

How a coach responds can be as fascinating as how quickly the person responds, but requires a bit more interpretation. I ended up having one or both of my parents read communications from coaches to see if the tone or content provided any insight about the level of interest or enthusiasm. Could the coach's reply be sent to any recruit (i.e., form letter, form email) or is it customized in any way? Does the coach comment about specific details provided in response to your message? If the response includes details, rest assured the coach probably read your correspondence carefully. In what does a coach take a particular interest: academics, athletics, community service, or something else? Such an emphasis may lend insight into his or her personal priorities. To what extent does the coach open up about the team or the attitudes of players? This may indicate the type of athletic personality for which he or she may be looking. Is it a short reply or a detailed and thoughtful response? The length of messages may lend insight into how busy the coach may be and the type of communication he or she likes to receive. When I received handwritten notes from a coach, I knew that he or she maintained a high degree of interest.

> **Primary point(s) of contact**

After receiving a response based on an initial contact, judge whether the head coach is the primary contact during recruiting. If nothing gets mentioned about that subject, then continue to communicate with the head coach. In several instances, a coach copied additional names on email replies. If they were not part of your initial correspondence, be sure to add the email addresses in your contact database and include them in future emails. In one instance, I was informed to send all future correspondence to an assistant coach, but copy the head coach on my email correspondence.

> **Special instructions**

On one Division I coach's initial reply, he gave instructions that all future correspondence should include LAST NAME, FIRST NAME, and COLLEGE GRADUATION CLASS in the subject line. This nomenclature corresponded to the system by which he organized and filed communications for each recruit. The instruction was a reasonable request and easy to follow. Special instructions such as this underscore the importance of reading *everything* you receive from coaches, and then being compliant and consistent in your communication with them! Not doing what they ask could be a sign indicating that you do not know how to follow instructions or do not care about their program.

> **Selectivity**

One Division I coach who communicated with me for two years indicated that over 500 prospective student-athletes had contacted him already for six spots on the team. Collegiate athletic recruiting is a highly selective process.

The push marketing campaign will give you some control over the process and convey valuable information about where you stand with a program at any given moment.

KEY SUMMARY POINTS:

> Push marketing entails expressing interest in a particular program by corresponding directly with a coach to present your credentials.

> An introduction to a coach includes your name, high school, year in high school, interest in his or her program, GPA, courses, awards and honors, training schedule, key statistics, upcoming competitions, and contact information.

> While Division I and II coaches are prohibited from responding to a recruit before the beginning of junior year and prohibited from contacting a recruit before the end of junior year, I recommend making contact as early as the end of freshman year of high school.

> One-page updates to coaches should be made when fresh information exists about athletic results, academic performance, community activities, and awards and honors.

CHAPTER 10: **NCAA ELIGIBILITY CENTER**

The National Collegiate Athletic Association (NCAA) Eligibility Center serves as both a part of pull marketing — by allowing recruits to set up a profile — and a requirement to be eligible to participate in a sport and earn scholarships. As recently as 2016, the NCAA called this service the NCAA Clearinghouse.

If you desire to participate in NCAA Division I or II athletics as a college freshman, "you must first register and be certified by the NCAA Initial-Eligibility Clearinghouse."[23] Athletes retain five years of athletic eligibility to compete for four years in college. For Division I athletes "to be eligible, students must: (1) graduate from high school, (2) maintain a 2.3-grade point average, and (3) complete a core curriculum of 16 academic subjects in high school."[24] The academic subjects represent full-year courses. A sliding scale is used among GPAs and standardized test scores to determine eligibility for Division I. Beginning in August 2018, Division II eligibility requires a 2.2 GPA with 14 courses in the core curriculum and an 820 combined reading and math score on the SAT or a 68 composite score on the ACT to compete as a college freshman. A 2.0 GPA is required in order to practice and be eligible for scholarships. Like

Division I, Division II also incorporates a sliding scale among GPA and standardized test scores to determine eligibility. While Division III schools are not bound by Eligibility Center certification requirements, a 3.0 average GPA in core courses and a 1000 SAT composite score or 86 composite score on the ACT are advised.

It is recommended that student-athletes register with the NCAA at the start of their junior year of high school. Students who fail to register with the NCAA or who do not meet minimum academic requirements "will not be eligible to play or practice" during their freshman year of college and lose one year of eligibility.[25] Student-athletes must be cleared by the NCAA before they can compete in their sport or receive a scholarship.

Athletes wanting to compete at the Division I or II collegiate level must register with the NCAA by completing five steps at NCAA.org/student-athletes/future/eligibility-center:

1. **Register.** Registration can be done anytime but must be completed by July 1 after your junior year of high school. Registering with the NCAA may not add you to coaches' recruiting lists, but it may drop you off of them if you fail to comply.

2. **Fill out a transcript release form.** A transcript release allows a high school to send a copy of your official transcript to the NCAA. Print and sign the release form.

3. **Request an official high school transcript.** A school representative must send the official transcript, not the athlete or parent. Deliver the signed form to the appropriate high school representative. Transcript information remains confidential.

4. **Request that testing services send scores to the NCAA.** Log onto the College Board (for SAT scores) or the ACT website and release a copy of your test score(s) to the NCAA. The NCAA

uses its own code, like each college or university. As of this writing, the NCAA code is 9999 for the SAT and ACT.

5. **Review the NCAA site to ensure that information gets submitted.** Return to the NCAA Eligibility Center website after several days, review your profile, and ensure that the NCAA received your registration, official transcript, and test scores for consideration and approval.

The NCAA Eligibility Center mailing address is P.O. Box 7136, Indianapolis, IN 46207. For U.S. callers with questions, contact the NCAA Eligibility Center customer service department at (877) 262-1492. International callers may call (317) 233-0700. Fees of $65 for U.S. and $75 for international athletes as of 2017 may be waived due to financial hardship. The National Association of Intercollegiate Athletics (NAIA) Eligibility Center, which follows a similar process to the NCAA, may be contacted at P.O. Box 15340, Kansas City, MO 64106.

Once your eligibility clears, you will be assigned an NCAA (or NAIA) eligibility number. This number is requested on individual school recruiting questionnaires and by coaches.

The question arises as to whether a recruit should become NCAA eligible if he or she is predominantly focused on Division III recruiting opportunities that do not require registration. First, you may not know whether a Division I program will demonstrate interest based on profiles featured in pull marketing recruiting websites. Four Division I programs and another four Division II programs expressed interest in my candidacy, even though I had not initially targeted any of them. I also targeted a handful of Division I programs with my push marketing campaign. If there is the possibility that even one Division I or Division II program may express interest, I highly recommend registering with the NCAA Eligibility Center. Consider all options throughout the collegiate athletic recruiting process. If nothing else, it serves as an additional profile accessible to coaches as part of a pull marketing strategy (see Chapter 8, Pull Marketing).

KEY SUMMARY POINTS:

› At the beginning of your junior year, apply for eligibility from the NCAA Eligibility Center.

› Compare your course curriculum, GPA, and standardized test scores to eligibility requirements by NCAA division to ensure that you remain eligible throughout the recruiting process.

CHAPTER 11: **RECRUITING QUESTIONNAIRES**

A recruiting questionnaire is a form that nearly every collegiate athletic program requires of a prospective recruit. On the team page for a respective college's website, a link usually prompts "Prospective Athletes" or "Prospective Recruit Questionnaire." Make sure you fill out the specific information for your sport and gender; questionnaires vary by sport depending upon what data a coach desires.

Recruiting questionnaires typically include contact information, address, statistics, and awards. Representative fields on a recruiting questionnaire for women's swimming at a small liberal arts college follow:

SAMPLE RECRUITING QUESTIONNAIRE FIELDS

General

First Name

Last Name

Email Address

Home Address 1

Home Address 2

City

State

Zip

Contact Number

Cell Phone Number

Date of Birth

Preferred Name

Ethnic Background (Optional)

Citizenship

Height

_____ Feet

_____ Inches

Gender

_____ Male

_____ Female

Résumé/Personal Profile (Upload)

Would you like financial aid information?

_____ Yes

_____ No

Profile Image (Upload)

Background

Mother's Name

Mother's Phone Number

Mother's Email Address

Mother's Alma Mater

Mother's Occupation

Father's Name

Father's Phone Number

Father's Email Address

Father's Alma Mater

Father's Occupation

Live with:

_____ Mother

_____ Father

_____ Both

Siblings Names, Ages, and Colleges, if appropriate

Family / Friends who have attended [College or University]

Academic

Graduation Year

High School/College

School Phone Number

Counselor's Name

Counselor's Phone Number

Class Rank

Grade Point Average (GPA)

SAT Math

SAT Critical Reading

SAT Writing

SAT Total

ACT

SAT II (i)

SAT II (ii)

Academic Honors

Transcript (Upload)

Intended Major

Other College Choices

Are you considering applying Early Decision?

_____ Yes

_____ No

Senior [Year] Courses

High School Profile

<u>Athletic</u>

YouTube Link

Club Team

Club Coach Name

Club Coach Phone

Club Coach Email

Club Coach Address

High School Coach Name

High School Coach Phone

High School Coach Email

Event(s)

_____ 50 freestyle

_____ 100 freestyle

_____ 200 freestyle

_____ 500/400 freestyle

_____ 1000/800 freestyle

_____ 1650/1500 freestyle

_____ 100 Backstroke

_____ 200 Backstroke

_____ 100 Breaststroke

_____ 200 Breaststroke

_____ 100 Butterfly

_____ 200 Butterfly

_____ 200 Individual Medley (IM)

_____ 400 Individual Medley (IM)

_____ One-meter Diving

_____ Two-meter Diving

Best Times and Scores (e.g., 00:00.00)

_____ 50 freestyle

_____ 100 freestyle

_____ 200 freestyle

_____ 500/400 freestyle

_____ 1000/800 freestyle

_____ 1650/1500 freestyle

_____ 100 Backstroke

_____ 200 Backstroke

_____ 100 Breaststroke

_____ 200 Breaststroke

_____ 100 Butterfly

_____ 200 Butterfly

_____ 200 Individual Medley (IM)

_____ 400 Individual Medley (IM)

_____ One-meter Diving (six dives)

_____ One-meter Diving (eleven dives)

_____ One-meter Diving (optional)

_____ Three-meter Diving (six dives)

_____ Three-meter Diving (eleven dives)

_____ Three-meter Diving (optional)

Anything else you would like us to know?

Each of these entries should be straightforward and will vary by sport, especially events and times. Filling out a recruiting questionnaire not only demonstrates an interest in a program but is required for recruitment. I am aware of a colleague in another sport who chose not to fill out an online recruiting questionnaire. As a result, the coach at that school no longer recruited the athlete and moved on to other prospects. If your information changes during the recruiting period, be sure to update the coach with new data.

While filling out online recruiting information demonstrates your recruiting interest in a particular program and may get you on a coach's radar, the questionnaire does not constitute interest by the program. The coach simply compiles information on a recruit. Coaches use various software products to build on these profiles and track all aspects involving a prospective student-athlete throughout the recruiting process. Most importantly, the coach quickly assesses whether you have a reasonable chance of earning admission to the college and whether you would contribute to the team. Therefore, recruiting questionnaires represent an early screen by which coaches determine whether to continue their interest in you, but not necessarily to recruit you.

Like profiles on recruiting websites in pull marketing, recruiting questionnaires are an important component of a successful push marketing campaign.

KEY SUMMARY POINTS:

›   Fill out a recruiting questionnaire for each team in which you are interested early in the recruiting process or as soon as a coach requests you to do so.

›   Update information and statistics on the questionnaire throughout the recruiting process.

CHAPTER 12: **ATHLETIC RÉSUMÉS AND VIDEOTAPES**

An athletic résumé represents another important push marketing tool for recruits. A well-constructed résumé provides college coaches with valuable information about a student-athlete's academic, athletic, and community accomplishments. Athletic résumés are better than recruiting questionnaires because you can include information relevant to you, include information not asked for in a recruiting questionnaire, feature key statistics that highlight your ability, personalize the résumé's design, and increase your exposure.

An athletic résumé should never exceed one page and typically involves up to eight components: personal contact information, objective, athletic profile, athletic statistics (e.g., best times, records, and relevant data), coaches' contact information, academic profile, community profile, and pictures:

› **Personal contact information** includes your name, home address, phone number, email address, and could also include height and weight. You can also include your NCAA Eligibility Number among personal information.

> **Objective** explains why you are interested in collegiate athletics. The objective is also an opportunity to call out any specific criteria in a college or university for which you are looking. On my athletic résumé, I included "winning team championships" in my objective.

> **Athletic profile** contains bullet point summaries of athletic accomplishments, awards, and captaincies. This information does not have to be limited to the sport for which you seek recruitment. College coaches always appreciate multi-sport athletes who become better in their particular sport. Athletic profile represents the section in which you establish the level of your athletic ability.

> **Athletic statistics** incorporate positions played, best times (e.g., swimming, cross country, track and field), season or career statistics (e.g., football, soccer, lacrosse, volleyball, ice hockey, field hockey, water polo), and records. The athletic statistics section attempts to give a coach concrete data to indicate whether you would make his or her team and how you might contribute to the team's success. In some instances, a coach may use such data to match a particular recruit (e.g., freestyle sprinter in swimming) to a specific recruiting need (e.g., freestyle anchor on relay teams).

> **Coaches' contact information** displays the name, organization, email address, and phone number for a club team or high school coach a college coach may want to contact on your behalf. An athletic résumé may also include the conference in which the club team or high school competes. For one school where I eventually took an official recruiting visit, the college coach contacted my club team swimming coach and conversed with him for an hour about my approach to swimming, accomplishments, and potential. My club team coach also spoke

with other college coaches that wanted me to swim for them, even though I ended up accepting official recruiting visits to other schools.

› **Academic profile** contains bullet-point summaries of academic information, including high school name, high school graduating class, class enrollment, unweighted and weighted GPA, class rank (if applicable), standardized test scores, AP and Honors courses taken or in progress, academic awards and scholarships, and academic membership societies. The academic profile section establishes that you have the credentials to get into the college or university. A coach does not want to spend precious time recruiting you if you cannot get past the admissions committee.

› **Community profile** contains bullet-point summaries of community and extracurricular involvement and awards.

› Array **photos** in different parts of the athletic résumé. Photos may include a school portrait and various images of a recruit in action.

With so many different aspects to convey in a profile, entries should involve bullet-points with only a few words each. A copy of my athletic résumé is provided to you as an example on scorecollegescholarships.com.

Design and arrange an athletic résumé that matches your unique style! Express yourself, but remember, keep it to one page and be honest!

Whereas individual sports like track and field, swimming, and tennis may lend themselves more to showcasing your accomplishments on an athletic résumé, certain individual sports (e.g., wrestling) and team sports (e.g., football, basketball, baseball, softball, soccer, ice hockey) involve highlighting skills on a video. Team sport coaches often ask for videos of a prospective recruit. That's because a video can better show your skill and ability, intensity, sportsmanship, team play, and game management. Like the athletic résumé, a video contains several components, including: a personal introduction, key statistics, video highlights — often emphasizing particular skills or capabilities — and a summary. Individual highlight videos may be sent to individual coaches and programs for their consideration.

Another opportunity is for a prospective student-athlete to set up a web presence on YouTube, Facebook, or other social medium. With a dedicated hub, newspaper articles and blogs in which your athletic exploits are featured may be posted.

An athletic résumé or video will get used throughout the recruiting process in a multitude of ways. It can be posted on-line to attract the interest of coaches, sent to coaches to summarize your profile, included as a part of pre-read materials for admissions offices before authorizing official recruiting visits, given to counselors and teachers making recommendations on your behalf, and appended to the college application where schools request an optional résumé or video.

Whether you choose to use an athletic résumé, video, and/or web presence, coaches want information that's summarized succinctly and compiled in one viewing.

KEY SUMMARY POINTS:

> A well-constructed athletic résumé provides college coaches with valuable information about your academic, community, and athletic accomplishments, including key statistics that highlight your ability.

> A skills video can showcase your skill and ability, intensity, sportsmanship, team play, and game management, particularly for team sports.

> An athletic résumé or video can be posted on-line, sent to coaches, included as a part of pre-read materials for admission, given to counselors and teachers making recommendations on your behalf, and appended to the college application.

CHAPTER 13: **RECRUITING AT SHOWCASES, CAMPS, CLINICS, AND COMPETITIONS**

Showcases typically involve high-level club team athletes at regional, state, or national levels. Depending on the team sport, a tournament features multiple games with top-flight talent. Institutional sports camps and clinics are "owned or operated by colleges or universities, or an employee of the institution's athletics department, either on or off campus, in which prospective student-athletes participate," according to the NCAA.[26] Spanning three days up to a week, showcases, camps, and clinics represent great opportunities for college coaches to scout talent.

A careful look at the *NCAA Guidelines for Camps and Clinics* provides an indication as to the purpose behind sports camps or clinics. Per Section 13.12.1.1.2:

"An institution's sports camp or clinic shall be one that:

a.   Places special emphasis on a particular sport or sports and provides specialized instruction or practice and may include competition;

b. Involves activities designed to improve overall skills and general knowledge in the sport; or

c. Offers a diversified experience without emphasis on instruction, practice or competition in any particular sport."[27]

No mention of recruiting — none. Recruiting does take place, however, at showcases, camps, and clinics by college coaches in attendance.

A further look at the NCAA Guidelines involving these types of recruiting activities sheds light on rules governing conduct and expectations. Section 13.12.1.6.1 states:

> "An institution, members of its staff, or representatives of its athletics interests shall not give free or reduced admission privileges to a high school, preparatory school, or two-year college athletics award winner or any individual being recruited by the institution…"[28]

Furthermore, Section 13.12.2.3.1 indicates:

> "No athletics department staff member may be employed… in any capacity by a camp or clinic established, sponsored, or conducted by an individual or organization that provides recruiting or scouting services concerning prospective student-athletes."[29]

A big misconception about showcases, camps, and clinics is that athletes will use them to get noticed by a coach — to get on a coach's radar. In reality, most coaches participating in these recruiting events have already identified prospects and attend to evaluate their performances, not to build a target list of recruits. The dilution of talent among participants reinforces this point in Section 13.12.1.3:

> "A member institution's sport camp or clinic shall be open to any and all entrants (limited only by number, gender and age)."[30]

Push marketing correspondence should always precede participation in a showcase, camp, clinic, or competition.

Coaches may also attend club or high school competitions. Assistant coaches from two different colleges attended different invitational swim meets where they could watch me compete. An email confirming their attendance, requesting an opportunity to get together after the event, and encouraging me beforehand indicated their degree of interest. One coach attended my state sectional championships meet. It helped that I anchored our medley relay team that won in come-from-behind fashion. Two coaches observed the USA Swimming Futures Championships at Stanford University in which I competed. If you have multiple coaches at the same event, be sure to manage your schedule so you can give each of them due attention.

KEY SUMMARY POINTS:

› Showcases, clinics, and camps represent tremendous ways to develop athletic skills against strong competition.

› Coaches are typically at a showcase, clinic, or camp to recruit other prospective student-athletes, not to build a target list of prospects.

CHAPTER 14: **CONTACT DATABASE**

A contact database may be the most important tool you use to stay organized throughout your collegiate athletic recruiting process. A contact database is nothing more than an Excel or similar spreadsheet program that a recruit updates to account for every contact made to a coach and every contact received from a coach or representative. Communicating with multiple coaches over the course of a two or three-year period makes it challenging to remember every contact made. Writing each correspondence down provides a resource to consult.

The contact database is your place to verify correct contact information, review information already sent to coaches, and analyze the amount, quality, and frequency of responses — a program's interest. The design of a contact database includes the following column headings:

› **College/University** includes the name of a college or university. Be sure to use the correct nomenclature in sending correspondence. For example, some smaller institutions in Division III from the same conference go by the name "university" (e.g., Wesleyan University) instead of "college" (e.g., Bowdoin College). Also be sure to account for "University of

X" as opposed to "X University." Even though they sport an "O-U" on their football helmets, the school in Norman, Oklahoma goes by the "University of Oklahoma." Likewise, even though they are known in Jayhawk Country as "K-U," it's the "University of Kansas." Paying attention to details in the eyes of a coach will signal that details matter to you.

› **Coach** identifies the preferred name of the head coach: "Coach X," "Mr. X," first name only, etc.

› **Assistant Coach(es)** lists all assistant coaches on the team, especially those copied on communications with the head coach.

› **Date** features the date of contact by a coach or recruit.

› **From** states who sent the message.

› **To** states who received the communication.

› **CC** or carbon copy lists who else was copied on the message.

› **Type** references the type of correspondence: email, text, phone call, letter, in-person meeting, etc.

› **Message summary** briefly summarizes the information conveyed. If it is an update as part of your push marketing, then include "Update #" with the key elements mentioned. Writing a short message will prevent you from having to slog through countless emails that accumulate throughout the recruiting process or find a particular piece of correspondence.

› **Questionnaire filled out?** This heading includes a date for when you filled out the team's online recruiting questionnaire or updated it (see Chapter 11, Recruiting Questionnaires).

> › **Athletic résumé or video submitted?** This column indicates the date on which you submitted an athletic résumé or video to the coach.

Download the blank Contact Database template and begin to enter the information gathered.

Entries get sorted by school and then chronologically so you can review all contact made and over what timeframe for a program under consideration. Filling out a contact database takes discipline every time a recruiting contact occurs. The effort will keep you organized and make sure communications are intentional, without omission or duplication.

Ultimately, whether and how a coach responds to your marketing efforts — including online profiles, recruiting questionnaires on the team's homepage, and correspondence — is everything! I had four college coaches email me immediately after I posted a profile on one swimming website. Two college coaches never bothered to respond — ever — after I filled out a recruiting questionnaire on their team's website and sent a personalized email introducing myself. You win some; you lose some. Developing and then assiduously filling out a contact database will help you keep track of correspondence and, more importantly, where you stand.

Communication needs to comply with NCAA Recruiting Guidelines and Rules, which Chapter 15 explores.

KEY SUMMARY POINTS:

› A contact database or spreadsheet helps you stay organized throughout the collegiate athletic recruiting process.

› By logging each contact to and from a coach, you can keep track of correspondence and assess where you stand as a recruit.

CHAPTER 15: **NCAA RECRUITING GUIDELINES AND RULES**

The NCAA produces a tome of regulations, guidelines, and rules governing the recruitment of prospective student-athletes. Rather than read all of this information yourself, or just rely on a coach and assume he or she is following the rules, following is a short synopsis produced by CollegeSportsScholarships.com of general guidelines to inform your contact with prospective coaches:[31]

NCAA RECRUITING GUIDELINES SUMMARY

High school freshman and sophomore year until September 1 of junior year:

› Recruits may:

   ○ Call or email coaches.

   ○ Make unofficial visits at their expense to a college campus (see Chapter 17, Unofficial Visits).

○ Talk with college coaches on campus, but not at camps or competitions.

› Coaches may:

○ Send NCAA educational information, questionnaires, and sports camp brochures from their institution.

○ Accept phone calls from prospective student-athletes at the recruit's expense.

› Coaches cannot:

○ Return messages left on answering machines.

○ Return emails.

○ Initiate calls to prospective student-athletes.

○ Send any written recruiting information.

High school junior year from September 1 through June 30:

› Coaches may:

○ Send written recruiting information about the school or program (e.g., media guides, personalized letters, and admissions publications).

○ Initiate emails to prospective recruits.

○ Respond to emails from prospective recruits.

High school junior year from July 1 until September 1 of senior year:

› Recruits may:

- ○ Call or email the coach as often as they wish.

› Coaches may:

- ○ Send written recruiting information about the school or program (e.g., media guides, personalized letters, and admissions publications).

- ○ Make one telephone call each week to a recruit or recruit's parent.

- ○ Contact recruit or recruit's parents in person off the college campus. Note: Coaches may make three in-person off-campus contacts throughout a recruitment.

High school senior year after the first day of classes:

› Recruits may:

- ○ Take up to five official recruiting visits of up to 48 hours in duration to Division I or II schools with expenses reimbursed. Note: Coaches require an official high school transcript and official SAT or ACT score before the visit.

› Coaches may:

- ○ Send written recruiting information about the school or program (e.g., media guides, personalized letters, and admissions publications).

- ○ Make one telephone call each week to a recruit or a recruit's parents.

See Collegesportsscholarships.com for more details about recruiting guidelines and rules. Chapters 17 and 19 contain additional rules about unofficial visits and official recruiting visits, respectively.

Recruiting guidelines keep changing. For example, as of this writing, the NCAA recently extended the timeframe for football recruits to take official visits beginning in the summer before senior year of high school. For additional information about updated recruiting guidelines, consult NCAA.org.

KEY SUMMARY POINTS:

› NCAA regulations at NCAA.org guide whether and how coaches correspond with recruits.

› NCAA guidelines do not preclude you from contacting coaches to introduce and update your academic and athletic qualifications any time as a prospective student-athlete.

SECTION IV: **TAKING CAMPUS VISITS**

CHAPTER 16: **TOURS AND INFORMATION SESSIONS**

Getting acquainted with a college or university involves taking campus tours and attending information sessions. Tours and information sessions may be pursued in conjunction with official recruiting visits, but in every experience, coaches provide specific itineraries for your visit that occupy all available time when you are on campus. If you want to explore a campus and get acquainted with it — outside of the world of recruiting — then I strongly recommend visiting the campus on a separate occasion, if your time and budget allow.

Campus tours involve more than spending an hour with a gregarious individual that walks backward, avoids every pole on campus, and seemingly knows everything about the school. Tours are typically student-led, 60- or 90-minute walking visits that convey information and provide a feel for a campus. While tours mainly serve prospective undergraduates, they accommodate prospective graduate students, prospective parents, members of the community, and members of higher education, teachers, and school guidance counselors interested in learning more about the institution. On a tour, participants see educational facilities, residences, and student accommodations. Campus tours typically take place Monday through Friday and selectively on weekends. Times vary. The content also varies markedly depending on the personality and knowledgeability of a guide. While seemingly difficult, it will be important not to let one tour guide overly affect — positively or adversely — your impression of the entire school.

An information session is typically a one-hour session facilitated by a member of the admissions staff for an undergraduate school. Information sessions take place on campus, or in locations throughout the country when a school conducts outreach and comes to a local hotel or high school. Information sessions attempt to convey the undergraduate experience, including specific aspects about residential life, extracurricular activities, research, internships, and academic advising. Every information session I attended spent a portion of the presentation on requirements for admission and recommendations for handling applications. In most cases, session leaders discussed financial aid information and provided references for how to get more information. While information sessions do not necessarily change your opinion about a school, they do provide an insight here and there about what to emphasize in your application and what to expect if admitted. I found it worth sitting through the approximately 60 minutes of information to capture "golden nuggets" you may use later in completing the application or making a decision about where to enroll. Multiple campus tours and information sessions are held throughout the day at many colleges and often occur concurrently so that participants migrate from the tour to the information session or vice-versa.

The timing about when to visit campuses, take tours, and attend information sessions presents a dilemma. Unlike visiting a property during a broker's open house when the owner abandons the place, the best time to visit a college campus is when the campus is bustling. It is often best to visit in the middle of the term, the middle of the week, and the middle of the day when students occupy campus. During the middle of the term, classes, activities, and social life are in full swing. Visit in the middle of the week because, on some weekends, a campus may empty when students go back home to family in the region or participate in weekend activities away from campus. You also want to visit in the middle of the day when campus life is vigorous. The conundrum remains that visiting in the middle of the week, or even in the middle of the day, requires missing high school classes. I ended up visiting campuses over the summer, during the two weeks my club team coaches gave off after the long-course swimming season ended and before high school started. Most college campuses were relatively deserted, but enough students and student activity gave me a reasonable impression of the schools. Decide for yourself how to weigh the trade-off between missing high school or missing athletic practices and competitions to see a college in full bloom.

If you are attempting to see multiple campuses in succession because you live out of the area or your schedule does not permit taking more time, you may have to make your own campus tour. Maps are readily available on all campuses, and with a little research and ingenuity, you can still develop a solid impression of a school. Campus video tours are available for over 1,700 colleges and universities through Campustours.com. If done in conjunction with an official visit, make sure that attending the campus tour and information session does not compromise what a coach or host intend for your recruiting visit.

Here are some guidelines based on my experience. First, schedule campus tours and information sessions. Registration takes place online or by calling the admissions office at the school. The more you show interest in a college, the more the admissions committee will look favorably upon you. Do not think for a moment that an admissions committee does not track every contact you may make with their institution; signing-up matters. Second, show up. Nothing will turn an admissions committee off more than you not showing up, or missing your scheduled time. The simplest of manners, like honoring your commitment and showing up for your campus tour or information session, will keep you in the running. Third, sign-in. The only way an admissions committee often knows if you did, in fact, show up is to look at the registry. Ask whether tour or information session participants need to sign-in. At one prestigious west coast college, the sign-in process was replete with a full-fledged survey about academic interests. They're tracking all of the information they can about you! Fourth, look presentable. While a suit and tie or formal dress would make you look silly and out-of-place, look like you care and want to attend the school. Effort counts, even with your appearance. Finally, ask a few thoughtful questions of your tour guide and information session leader.

Following is a list of the kinds of questions to prepare in advance before your visit:

›   Questions for Leader of Campus Tour

   o   Why did you choose [College or University]?

   o   What one thing would you like to change about [College or University]?

›   Questions for Leader of Information Session

   o   What future priorities or changes, if any, does [College or University] plan?

   o   Is there an early read process for recruited athletes and how does that work?

At the end of a campus tour or information session, be sure to get contact information from the guide or session leader. That evening or upon returning home, write a thank you letter or email to your tour guide and information session leader. Here is a sample thank you letter I emailed to a tour guide:

From: Laura Dickinson '17
Sent: Friday, August 14, 2015 8:49 PM
To: [Tour Guide]
Subject: Thank You

Dear [Tour Guide],

Thank you for taking the time on Monday, August 10th to share your insights and speak with me about [College]. Having just completed a visit to sixteen college campuses in eight days, I can say with a genuine perspective that [College or University] stands at the top of my list of colleges and universities.

In particular, I enjoyed hearing about the many languages offered and seeing the impressive athletic facilities. As a competitive swimmer nationally, getting to tour the aquatics facility confirmed my interest in [College].

I look forward to returning to [College] for a more comprehensive tour or even a recruiting visit after my junior year at [High School]. Thank you again for sharing your passion and helpful information about [College].

Sincerely,

Laura Dickinson

Following is a sample thank you letter I mailed to an admissions representative conducting an information session off-campus:

August 15, 2015
[Dean]
Senior Assistant Dean of Admission
[College or University]

Dear [Dean],

Thank you for taking the time to co-facilitate the [College or University] information session for prospective applicants at the Hyatt Regency in San Francisco today. Having taken a self-guided tour of [College or University] on August 6, 2013, I can picture the benefits of the [Amenities] you described.

In particular, I enjoyed hearing about how liberal arts at [College or University] won't prepare one for any particular job, but for every job, and that most jobs in ten years do not exist today. I also learned about the importance of relationships with professors and peers, put into practice through sponsor groups of fifteen students living together.

As a competitive swimmer nationally, [Coach] of the [College or University] women's swimming team and I have been in consistent contact for over a year. I look forward to returning to [College or University] for a more comprehensive tour or even a recruiting visit after my junior year at [High School].

Thank you again for sharing your passion and helpful information about [College or University].

Sincerely,

Laura Dickinson

Why does writing a thank you letter matter? While the tour guide or information session leader may not decide whether you get in, he or she reports back to admissions on a prospective student's level of interest, appearance, behavior, and questions asked. Most notes or comments go straight into the personal file that the admissions committee creates about you. In addition, following up is a skill that matters when applying for jobs in the working world.

Campus tours and information sessions present a useful way to help decide whether to even pursue a school. I visited 16 colleges and universities on a Northeastern and Mid-Atlantic trip during the summer between sophomore and junior years of high school. After I concluded that the environment surrounding one campus was not for me, I completed my visit after only six minutes! Of the 16 schools, all of which looked attractive on paper, I dropped half from consideration. It may have been my best use of time during the collegiate athletic recruiting process, not having to pursue or apply to schools I would not want to attend. Ironically, after receiving or initiating 52 inquiries from collegiate coaches, I ended up enrolling at the school to which I made my very first campus visit.

At some schools, prospective students get assigned a school admissions representative by region, and in some cases, by high school. Colleges make a point of understanding schools within a geographic area. By following the applicants from the same high schools year-after-year, they have a better chance of assessing an individual candidate and the pool of candidates from a given high school and area. Find out who may be the regional or school admissions contact before leaving campus. I sent the following sample letter to one such admissions representative immediately following my campus tour and information session:

April 3, 2016
[Mr. Associate Director]
Associate Director of Admissions
Office of College Admissions
The University of [College or University]

Dear [Associate Director]:

My name is Laura Dickinson, and I am a high school junior at [High School] in [City]. On Tuesday, I enjoyed a welcoming, informative, and inspiring visit to the [College or University].

Upon arriving on campus, I participated in an information session, campus tour, and unofficial recruiting visit with a varsity coach. At [Campus Building], [Student A] greeted me warmly and brought me to the information session, and [Student B] guided an entertaining and personable tour of campus. In particular, I learned about the benefits of the Core curriculum, flexibility in the housing program, and rivalries that take place among houses. Hearing about [College or University] traditions, including the annual four-day [Excursion], the [Contest], and [Activity] on Wednesdays filled me with excitement. My tour guide also offered personal tips for how to be successful not only at [School] but any college or university. As a prospective student-athlete, I met at the [Athletic Center] with [Coach], the [College or University] women's swimming head coach. Attached please find a copy of my athletic résumé for your reference.

Some students know what subjects they want to study. I see college as something different: the potential for countless surprises representing new knowledge and personal growth exists. I want my college experience to prepare me to be a good citizen, to teach me how to think critically and uncover a better sense of myself. I believe that [College or University] will fulfill that for me because I can explore the Core curriculum, pursue the depth of the major I choose and contribute to a nationally-competitive women's swimming team at the same time.

Having toured several colleges and universities around the country and conducted unofficial recruiting visits to three, I can say with conviction that [College or University] stands at the top of my list! I look forward to applying to the university and returning to [College or University] for what I hope will be an official recruiting visit and interview next fall.

Sincerely,

Laura Dickinson

My advice would be to start visiting campuses in your freshman year of high school. When your family goes on vacation, and there may be a college in which you might be interested nearby, take an hour or two to drop in and experience the campus. After competing in an invitational swim meet a few hours from our home, my mother and I took a walking tour of a college campus near the pool. Even without a formal campus tour or information session, I gleaned enough valuable information about the school to consider it further.

Getting the chance to see what may be your home for four critical years of your life can be exhilarating! While you cannot feasibly tour every institution, the ones in which you are interested, or even the ones to which you end up applying, taking as many campus tours and participating in as many information sessions as reasonably possible can help you identify a good fit.

KEY SUMMARY POINTS:

› Taking campus tours and attending information sessions represent a great way to become acquainted with a college campus outside of the recruiting process.

› Information gleaned at tours and information sessions can be used to evaluate whether to continue pursuing a school and how to position your application for admission.

› Schedule tours and sessions, prepare thoughtful questions to ask, and send thank you notes to your tour guides and session leaders.

CHAPTER 17: **UNOFFICIAL VISITS**

Another way to identify a good fit is to take an unofficial visit to a school. According to the NCAA, "any visit by you and your parents to a college campus paid for by you or your parents" constitutes an unofficial visit.[32] In effect, a prospective student-athlete is demonstrating a keen interest in a particular school and program by initiating an unofficial visit.

There are several reasons why an unofficial visit makes sense. First, you may want to get a jump on the process and evaluate whether to continue pursuing a program. Second, a coach may not have decided whether to invite you for an official visit (see Chapter 19: Official Recruiting Visits). Finding the time, making an effort, and footing the bill may move recruiting with that particular program forward. Third, official visits often do not take place before the beginning of the student-athlete's senior year of high school. As some "college coaches [recruit prospects] during their freshman and sophomore years in high school, the only way they can [meet and talk] with these recruits is on unofficial visits."[33] Finally, you may take as many unofficial visits as you would like.

According to ESPN.com, "unofficial visits have become the

currency of today's college ... recruiting world. They keep the modern recruiting machine running all year long."[34] By the end of August, before the start of senior year for the 2013 recruiting class, 225 of the top 300 football recruits around the country had already committed to programs. This statistic means that 75% committed early and did not wait for a single official recruiting visit. Unofficial visits were used to inform their decision.

Reuben Foster, a top ten football recruit, made 20 unofficial visits during his junior year of high school before ending up at Auburn University. Maurice Smith, a top 150 cornerback prospect from Texas, took 15 unofficial visits to eight different schools before deciding on Alabama. I made two unofficial visits during the spring break of my junior year in high school.

Before making an unofficial visit, be sure to reach out to the coach to communicate your intention and plans, like the email exchange that follows:

From: Laura Dickinson
Sent: Tuesday, January 26, 2016 2:42 PM
To: [Coach]
Subject: Campus Visit

Hi [Coach],

Toward the end of December, we exchanged emails. I mentioned wanting to visit the [College or University] during my spring break and you expressed an interest in getting together.

I'm in the process of planning a couple of days off from swim practices to get to [City]. At this point, I could arrive at

[Airport] on Tuesday, March 29th shortly after noon and depart Wednesday, March 30th around 1 p.m.

Would you be available to meet either mid- to late-afternoon on Tuesday the 29th or the morning of Wednesday the 30th?

[College or University] offers an information session at 2 p.m. and tour at 3 p.m. on Tuesday, and information session at 9 a.m. and tour at 10 a.m. on Wednesday.

Please let me know your interest and availability at your convenience.

Thanks,

Laura

From: [Coach]
Date: January 28, 2016 at 12:26:30 PM PST
To: Laura Dickinson
Cc: [Assistant Coach]
Subject: RE: Campus Visit

Hi, Laura!

I'm excited that you will be coming out for a visit in March. I am available to meet with you Tuesday until 4 pm and on Wednesday any time after 10 am. Let me know what works best for you and when you plan on stopping by. I look forward to meeting you soon!

[Coach]

One unofficial visit involved a top academic school in the Midwest that constitutes a "reach" for every applicant. I met with the head coach for an hour, met with an assistant coach, toured the natatorium and campus, and attended an information session. The other unofficial visit involved a prominent Northeastern liberal arts college that constitutes a "reach" for most applicants. During the unofficial visit, I had a one-hour meeting with the coach, toured the campus, and attended an information session. The coach indicated that he could get me into the college if my credentials appeared to be a slam-dunk for admissions.

Make unofficial visits, in my estimation, after you conduct your academic and athletic qualifications research about the program, decide that the school and team would make an appropriate fit for you, and conclude that the program is a top priority. Also, undertake unofficial visits after determining that you are at least on a coach's watch list. It would make little sense to conduct an unofficial visit if the coach never returned your initial correspondence or did not show enthusiasm in his or her responses to your contacts. In my two cases, I had emailed with the head coach for a year-and-a-half on at least a quarterly basis about my interest. An unofficial visit also does not make sense unless you contact the coach and see whether he or she would be interested in your stopping by for a visit and meeting. Ideally, the coach either asks you to visit the school, or you ask and receive an indication that you should visit.

Unlike official recruiting visits, unofficial visits do not involve staying with a host student-athlete, interacting extensively with the team, or necessarily conducting a thorough visit. The extent to which a coach is willing to schedule a meeting, set up an itinerary, and arrange for you to meet some of the team members on an unofficial visit, however, goes a long way to understanding to what extent a coach may be interested in you. Recruits do not stay with a team member because a prospect may not receive cost-free housing on an unofficial visit. Both coaches on my unofficial visits expressed keen interest in my stopping by, but made it clear that my pre-read materials would determine whether recruitment would continue and that admissions made all final decisions. You can also ask a coach for a pre-read before making an unofficial visit, but in all likelihood, there exists a short track record of high school grades on your transcript, standardized tests remain untaken, and the coach may not be prepared yet to sit down with a representative from admissions.

The NCAA maintains strict regulations about unofficial visits involving the prospective recruit and parents as follows:[35,36]

NCAA Unofficial Visit Guidelines

Definition	An unofficial visit is a visit financed entirely by the recruit.
Number Permitted	A recruit may take an unlimited number of unofficial visits to an institution.
First Opportunity to Visit	Unofficial visits may take place at any time, except during a dead recruiting period.
Documentation Before a Prospect Makes a Visit (e.g., test scores, transcripts, NCAA verification)	No documentation is required.
Length of the Visit	An unofficial visit may take place for an unlimited duration.
Transportation	Transportation expenses may not be provided by an institution or program to a recruit, except for: Transportation to view practice and competition sites. Local transportation to attend a home athletics event.
Parking	Paid parking may not be provided by an institution or program.

Lodging	Cost-free housing may not be provided by an institution or program.
Meals	Meals may not be provided by an institution or program.
Entertainment	Entertainment may not be provided by an institution or program.
Complimentary Admissions	An institution or program may provide a recruit with three complimentary admissions to a home athletics event.
Recreational Activities	Participation in recreational activities is allowed, as long as activities are neither organized nor observed by members of the athletic department. Activities may not be designed to test a recruit's abilities. Any facility used must be open to the general public.
Publicity	An institution or program may not publicize a recruit's visit to campus.

For both unofficial visits and official recruiting visits, recruits should be prepared with questions to ask coaches to make the most of the visit:

Questions to Coaches

> Goals: What are your goals for the [gender/sport] team?

> Culture: Describe the culture of the team.

> Student-Athlete Balance: How are athletics and academics balanced and supported (e.g., schedules to accommodate practices, study hall, tutors if necessary)?

> Recruitment: Based on my profile, how would you envision my helping the team?

› Admissions: What represents the typical profile of [gender/ sport] recruits admitted?

› Application Type: What expectations do you have for recruits as to when they apply (e.g., Early Decision, Early Action, Regular Decision)?

› Coaching Assistance: What leverage, if any, do you have with the admissions office for recruits?

› Process: Describe the recruiting process from here (e.g., pre-read, official recruiting visit, decisions).

The following lists actual questions I received during recruiting visits:

Questions for Recruit

› What are you looking for in a college [sport] program?

› Why do you want to come to [College or University]?

› What would you want to study?

› What kind of [athlete] are you?

　○ What has your training been?

　○ What coaching style suits you best?

　○ What kind of teammate are you?

　○ Describe a good teammate.

› What is your greatest [athletic] accomplishment?

› What other schools are recruiting you?

› What other schools are you considering?

Unofficial visits are best for schools and programs in which you are most interested and want to increase your chances of receiving an official invitation for a recruiting visit. A recruit can learn tremendous insights about the coach, but less so about the team dynamic and culture, in the process. The other advantage about an unofficial visit is that you can mention it in your pre-read materials for admissions and on the application to the college which underscores your tremendous interest in the potential opportunity. As ESPN.com states about recruits and their families paying for the privilege to get in front of a coach, "the opportunity to get recruited is a rare and incomparable experience. Just don't call it priceless."[37]

KEY SUMMARY POINTS:

› An unofficial visit, paid for by a recruit and often taken prior to senior year, demonstrates a keen interest in a college team.

› Conduct an unofficial visit only after conducting research about the school, determining if it would be an appropriate fit, communicating with a coach, and receiving his or her permission to do so.

› Prepare questions for the coach, be prepared to answer questions from the coach, comply with NCAA guidelines about unofficial visits, and send thank you notes after your unofficial visit.

CHAPTER 18: **PRE-READS**

Pre-reads establish a gateway to determine whether a prospective student-athlete may make it past the admissions committee on a certain campus. A pre-read involves a recruit sending documentation about transcripts, standardized test results, and other information requested by a coach — and the coach sitting down with a representative from admissions to review a recruit's qualifications. Prospective student-athletes do not attend pre-reads.

The last thing a coach wants to do is waste precious time and budget pursuing a recruit who cannot get admitted to the school, and a recruit does not want to chase an opportunity that will not come to fruition. In multiple cases, coaches would signal a "green light" (i.e., you will probably get into the school), "yellow light" (i.e., there is something about your qualifications that lends doubt about whether you get in), or "red light" (i.e., time to move on to other options and recruits) to characterize feedback from admissions. The feedback determines whether the coach extends one of a limited number of competitive official recruiting visit invitations.

Because coaches conduct official recruiting visits during the fall of a recruit's senior year of high school, they need to carefully select whom to invite. For a coach to determine whom to invite and confirm visits, he or she needs to start extending offers over the summer between the junior and senior years of high school for a recruiting class. Therefore, pre-read materials are requested as early as May and typically in June or July at the end of the junior year after final high school grades have posted.

If a coach requests pre-read materials, you are clearly on his or her recruiting radar, subject to feedback from admissions. I had 16 coaches solicit pre-read materials, 11 in whose programs I was interested, like the email below:

From: [Admissions]
Date: July 14, 2016 at 11:00:17 AM PDT
To: Laura Dickinson
Subject: [College or University] - Transcript Request

Hi Laura,

Good afternoon! I hope you are enjoying your summer!

I am reaching out because we have the opportunity to have your transcript reviewed by admissions to see how **[College or University]** may fit into your college search. It is a unique opportunity, and I would love to help you out with it.

Also, just to be clear, this is a very important step for us in the recruiting process.

Would you please send me an unofficial transcript with all grades from freshman through junior year? I will pass it along for a pre-read and let you know when I hear back.

Thank you!

[Coach]

Most coaches only required unofficial copies of transcripts with grades through junior year and printouts of standardized test scores from a testing agency's website — numbers to plug into an admissions formula to determine the attractiveness of a prospective candidate academically.

Five coaches also requested a school profile — a report which is produced by high school staff summarizing the size, educational offerings, and statistics about your current high school.

What a tremendous opportunity! A coach at a school and program in which you are interested will sit down with a decision-maker from admissions to review your qualifications! The feedback from such a conversation informs whether you should apply to the school, and if you apply, whether you can get in. Whereas the coach may only ask for numbers — a transcript and standardized test scores — I recommend sending as much information as possible without overwhelming the coach or admissions staff. Coaches generally sit down with an admissions representative once. If a coach is going to receive feedback from admissions, he or she wants to receive the most informed decision possible. Why not send as much about what you will feature in your application, short of sending in the application itself? You might as well give them as complete a picture of your credentials and qualifications as possible. In all 11 cases where I sent pre-read materials to a collegiate coach, I included:

a. Official transcript with grades through junior year

b. SAT or ACT standardized test scores

c. SAT II Subject test scores

d. High school profile

e. Senior year class schedule

f. Graded writing sample

g. Common Application or Coalition Application essay draft

h. Supplemental essay drafts, if available

i. One-page athletic résumé (including academic and community information)

j. Key athletic statistics (e.g., best times progression in swimming)

Every coach appreciated receiving the additional information. Sending draft application essays demonstrates a commitment to the school and compiling a comprehensive package reflects good organizational skills. In most cases, pre-read materials should be sent by July 1 between junior and senior year of high school.

A recruit may receive pre-read requests from individual coaches and radio silence from other coaches in whose institutions you still maintain an interest, if not the highest priority. In response to pre-read requests from coaches, a recruit should compile and send relevant information along with a cover letter or email. To solicit a pre-read from a coach, do the same thing. In every case in which I did not receive a pre-read request and knew the coach had some interest in me, he or she promptly agreed to conduct a pre-read. If a coach receives useful information about you as a viable recruit, you are making his or her job that much easier. Content in the following letter reflects not only a response to a pre-read request but a request for a pre-read:

June 27, 2016
Head Swimming Coach
[College or University]
[Address]
[City, State, Zip]
RE: Laura Dickinson '21 Recruiting Profile

Dear [Coach]:

Entering the recruiting season for the Class of 2021, I would like to reiterate that [College or University] and your Women's Swimming and Diving program stand at the very top of my list among school options. I took a self-guided tour of [College or University] on August 9, 2015, and returned to campus for an information session led by [Session Leader], a campus tour guided by [Student-Athlete], and a meeting with you on March 31, 2016. More importantly, I appreciate having had the chance to correspond with you via email several times since August, 2014 about [College or University] women's swimming and my progress in the classroom and in the pool. As an undecided major and competitive swimmer, I believe that [College or University] open curriculum , women's swimming team, and balanced approach to academics, athletics, and service afford me the best opportunity to flourish in college.

I would like to provide a recruiting profile containing athletic and academic information for your consideration:

Résumé. The first attachment is a one-page résumé summarizing my athletic, academic, and community service qualifications.

Swimming Qualifications. The second attachment includes a best-times progression among selected swimming strokes. At the 2016 [Conference] Women's Swimming Championships, I would be able to score in 7 individual events among 3 different strokes plus relays based on personal best times.

[High School] Profile. Attached as the third document is the most recently published school profile for [High School], including available AP/Honors courses, GPA distribution, and test score averages.

Transcripts. Two sets of transcripts are provided: the fourth attachment is my unofficial [High School] transcript for grades nine through eleven and the fifth attachment is a [School Name] High School transcript for a class I took in eighth grade. My combined cumulative GPA across all high school courses, including pluses and minuses, is a [GPA] weighted and [GPA] unweighted, despite missing 41 classes this past spring semester for travel meets.

Standardized Test Scores (ACT, SAT II). The sixth attachment includes ACT scores. The seventh attachment includes a [Score] SAT II Subject Test score in French.

Senior Year Class Schedule. Attached as the eighth document is my four-year high school class schedule, including senior year courses highlighted in yellow.

Graded Writing and Poetry Samples. Finally, I include graded writing and poetry samples as attachments nine and ten to provide a sense of my analytical and writing ability. [College] requests a writing sample as part of its Common Application supplement.

I wanted to provide you with as complete a profile as possible so you can determine whether I would be an appropriate fit for [College or University] and your Women's Swimming Program and whether I would be a candidate for a Recruiting Weekend visit this fall. If there is anything else I can provide, please let me know.

This summer, I am training 11 practices per week with [Team

or Persons] and getting ready for the USA Swimming Futures meet in Palo Alto this August.

Thank you for your consideration. I look forward to hearing from you upon your return from vacation.

Sincerely,

Laura Dickinson

In addition to reaching out to coaches at programs in which you are interested that have not requested a pre-read, plan your recruiting schedule to complete all standardized tests — and receive scores to your liking — by the end of your junior year of high school. As highlights in the following email illustrate, despite increasing standardized test scores during the first test sitting of my senior year, all official recruiting visit spots at one university were already filled:

From: [Head Coach]
Date: September 30, 2016 at 8:30:11 AM PDT
To: Laura Dickinson '17
Cc: [Assistant Coach]
Subject: RE: Update

Nice job, Laura! That score definitely makes you a much more competitive applicant, however, I still cannot give you any type of guarantee in terms of admissions. All of our fall recruiting weekends are full but you are welcome to visit on your own any time that works for you. Depending on how EA goes, maybe we can have you come out for a visit in January.

[Head Coach]

If this doesn't convince you to take standardized tests and achieve satisfactory scores by the end of your junior year, I do not know what would!

I believed that pre-reads would be the most important aspect of my recruiting process. Coaches cannot guarantee admissions; only the admissions office may do so. Below I have included a sample response from a coach candidly and directly providing "red light" pre-read feedback:

From: [Coach]
Date: July 20, 2016 at 11:46:22 AM PDT
To: Laura Dickinson '17
Subject: read

Laura,

I just received feedback from our admissions office regarding your pre-read. Based on the information I submitted on your behalf and my overall recruiting picture, I will not be able to support your application if you decide to apply to [College]. I wish I was sending better news but I want to be honest with you. If you have any questions at all please let me know and I am happy discussing them with you.

Take care,

[Coach]

The operative words in the coach's response are "…and my overall recruiting picture." The fact that only admissions may guarantee acceptance into a school may be used as a shield to protect the coach from giving straight-talk about your recruitment chances. Coaches might veil reality or delay results to see whether better recruits come along.

One coach reiterated a "yellow light" even before the pre-read took place:

From: [Head Coach]
Date: July 1, 2016 at 4:23:33 AM PDT
To: "Laura Dickinson '17
Subject: Re: Laura Dickinson '21 Recruiting Profile

Laura -

Thanks very much for the note and for providing me so much information, it's very helpful. I will certainly send this through admissions once our liaison returns in the middle of July.

At this point the swimming and transcript look pretty good, I'm just wondering if you have taken the ACT again or are planning to. I would say at this point that is likely the one item that is outside of the range for [College or University].

Keep me posted on that, in addition it would be great to hear a little about your college search. What are you ultimately looking for in a school and what schools are at the top of your list at the moment?

Thanks and keep us posted, I look forward to continuing the conversation!

[Coach]

In this correspondence, the coach probably wonders if his college is the only school I am considering, or if it represents my top choice.

For another coach providing mixed "yellow light" reviews from admissions, deciding whether and how to proceed with the program became more complicated for me as evidenced by the email following:

From: [Head Coach]
Date: July 19, 2016 at 4:40:36 PM PDT
To: "Laura Dickinson '17"
Subject: Admissions update

Laura,

I wanted to let you know I was able to meet with our admissions office this past week regarding your academic profile. Based on your current academic info and our interest in you as a swimmer, you fall right on the line of acceptance; meaning, if you were to apply ED and I was to support your application, I'm not sure whether I could make the difference and help you earn admission to [College or University]. Your transcript looks great but you current testing is holding you back; I believe with improvement you'd be in a good position to apply early and be admitted to [College or University]. Putting together a strong senior year will be necessary as well. I won't be able to make any projections about an admissions decision to [College or University] now but when you receive updated testing we can revisit if you remain serious about [College or University] being a top choice school for you. I don't want to discourage you from considering [College or University] but do want to give you honest feedback on where you stand. If you'd like to talk more about it please let me know and we can connect over the phone.

Best,

[Coach]

By linking chances of acceptance with applying Early Decision, this coach appears to be trying to extract a greater commitment to his program.

Admissions committees conferring "green lights" and coaches offering official visit invitations fueled my esteem:

From: [Head Coach]
Date: July 29, 2016 at 10:00:14 AM PDT
To: "Laura Dickinson '17"
Subject: Re: Laura Dickinson '21 Recruiting Profile

Hi Laura,

Apologies for the long delay. After four weeks of swim camps and two weeks traveling [Cities] I finally have a little time back in the office to catch up.

So I had a great conversation with admissions about you and your pre-read. They were very impressed and hope that you will remain interested. They essentially gave me the green light for next steps... like a visit this fall? Let me just take a second to say thank you for all your effort in the classroom and life. It makes my role a lot easier when I present such great people to admissions.

Again, the lack of contact doesn't reflect a lack of interest just a crazy five weeks. I hope you are doing well, I would love to hear from you. Maybe you are at [Meet]? Or going to something soon? I will see what I can find instead of asking you random questions on email. Anyway, I look forward to hearing back from you.

Take care,

[Coach]

Here's another "green light" example reflecting positive pre-read results:

From: [Coach]
Date: July 19, 2016 at 8:44:27 PM PDT
To: Laura Dickinson '17
Subject: [College or University] **recruit invite**

Hi Laura

As we've engaged in the recruiting process for the [College] class of 2021, you have emerged as a strong academic and athletic fit with our program. Based on your strengths, we **invite you** to one of our **Recruit Weekends**...Oct 6-8 or Oct 20-22, 2016

Please see the attached pdf for more details and respond as soon as possible.

Stay in touch and

Go [Team]!

[Coach]

In my experience, at the one test-optional school to which I applied, the coach offered guidance about which test scores I should submit with my application based on feedback he received from admissions during the pre-read.

The only complication at this point involves juggling multiple recruiting visit offers without exceeding the NCAA limit, avoiding scheduling conflicts, and missing too much high school.

KEY SUMMARY POINTS:

› As a prerequisite to an official visit invitation, a pre-read determines whether admissions staff at a college or university will look favorably upon a prospective student-athlete for admission.

> Whereas a coach will typically request submission of your official transcript and standardized test scores, I also recommend submitting any information (e.g., SAT II Subject test scores, high school profile, senior year class schedule, graded writing sample, application essay drafts, athletic résumé, and key athletic statistics) that will give admissions staff a full representation of your candidacy.

CHAPTER 19: **OFFICIAL RECRUITING VISITS**

You have established communications with a coach, received a "green light" from admissions to continue, and now the only thing standing between you and fulfilling your dream of participating in a collegiate sport at a desired school is passing the "fit test" with prospective teammates and coaches. An official recruiting visit represents an important element in the recruiting process before making a decision.

In most cases, there exist a limited number of spots for prospective recruits. While the number of recruits hosted will vary by program and sport, the programs I visited hosted between six and eight athletes from around the country each recruiting weekend. Hosting two recruiting weekends, most swim programs I encountered evaluated up to 16 prospective recruits for a few spots on each team. Getting an official recruiting visit invitation is indeed competitive, and the visits themselves are vital!

Some prospective student-athletes may receive more official visit invitations to campuses than they can experience. The NCAA limits the number of official visits to five schools for Division I and/or Division II, allows unlimited visits to Division III and NAIA programs, and limits a recruit to one official visit per school. I found that time is a finite resource during a busy fall of your senior year taking a full course load and filling out college applications. If you are in the advantageous position of receiving multiple official visit invitations, select your recruiting visits carefully. When scheduling multiple visits, see which weekends conflict across schools. Keep options open as much as possible because not all coaches will extend invitations at the same time. All but one of the programs I pursued conducted official recruiting visits over two weekends; the other program hosted five recruiting weekends.

For example, I received official visit offers from three schools initially. School A offered weekends one and three, School B offered weekends one and four, and School C offered weekends two and six. I consulted my high school and athletic schedules to determine if any of these weekends should be ruled out. It turned out that weekend three involved an important invitational swim meet already on my schedule. Weekend one presented a conflict between Schools A and B. Based on these considerations, I penciled in weekend one for School A, weekend four for School B, and weekend two for School C, wanting to complete all official recruiting visits as early as possible. Several days later, I received one more official visit invitation from School D on weekends two and three. Because I had an athletic conflict on weekend three, I would have to select weekend two for School D. Having already penciled in weekend two for School C, I changed this visit on my plan to weekend six. I now planned for School A on weekend one, School D on weekend two, School B on weekend four, and School C on weekend six.

Aside from pure scheduling, another thing to consider about responding to official visit invitations involves your initial preferences among schools. I know of one prospect who scheduled her first school choice for the first official visit. Loving what she experienced on that visit, she accepted the coach's offer, canceled subsequent recruiting visits, and completed her recruiting journey. I know of another prospect who scheduled her preferred school last among official visits to give other options a fair and impartial evaluation. In my experience, I scheduled visits over a one-to-two-week timeframe as coaches offered them. I believed that a coach from a high-quality school and well-regarded program reaching out before other coaches deserved stronger consideration; an early inviter must have an interest in my joining the team. After all, you may not receive additional official visit invitations. If all other variables remain equal and coaches extend invitations about the same time, try to respond promptly.

If conflicting dates do arise, you may always contact a coach and see whether additional or alternative weekends can be made available to accommodate your schedule. Doing so because of high school or athletic conflicts will be received more favorably, however, than because you already signed up for another collegiate coaches' official recruiting weekend. If a coach remains serious, he or she may make a visit to your family home.

Official recruiting visits signify that a coach is investing more than just time in a prospective student-athlete. The coach invests money, possibly for airfare, transportation, lodging, and meals; the time of members on the team; and his or her reputation bringing in a prospect no one else in the program has probably met to this point. For these reasons, take official recruiting visits very seriously!

I found that it is a good idea to make and communicate travel plans with the coach before confirming airline reservations. All four of my official recruiting visits involved roundtrip flights. In each case, I made a reservation that spanned 48 hours, arriving and leaving on the days a coach specified in the invitation. I then sent the preliminary itinerary to the coach to confirm that it worked before booking the flights. I wanted to make sure the itinerary complied with NCAA regulations, and that pick-up and travel from the airport to campus and back matched the coach's expectations. Traveling from the west coast on a red-eye flight to the Northeast, I arrived for one visit around 5:00 a.m. If a current team member is assigned to pick you up from the airport, you want to make sure that kind of arrival time works. Often, coaches may be picking up multiple recruits with similar arrival times, so it makes sense to check-in before booking non-refundable airfare.

Once an official visit is scheduled, a coach typically provides an itinerary from arrival at the airport or to the campus through your departure from campus. The itinerary identifies who will pick you up or how to arrange transportation from the airport, with whom you will be lodging, and activities throughout your stay, including team practice attendance, entertainment, classes, and meetings with admissions representatives, academic advisors, professors, and coaches.

When a coach sends you an itinerary, he or she may also send you a form from the NCAA to be filled out, signed, and returned before your arrival on campus.

Coaches may also send an institution-specific form for completion and signature.

NCAA Bylaw 13.6 which follows, complete rules and regulations regarding official recruiting visits:[38]

NCAA Official Visit Guidelines

Definition	An official visit is a visit financed in part or in whole by the institution.
Number Permitted	A prospect may take a maximum of five expense-paid visits. This applies to Division I and/or Division II programs. Unlimited visits are allowed to Division III and NAIA programs. No more than one visit is permitted to any single institution.

First Opportunity to Visit	The first opportunity to visit occurs on the first day of classes for a recruit's senior year of high school.
Documentation Before a Prospect Makes a Visit (e.g., test scores, transcripts, NCAA verification)	An institution must receive: > Valid PSAT, SAT, PLAN, or ACT score, > Official high school transcript, > Verification of registration with NCAA Eligibility Center.
Length of the Visit	The length of the visit cannot exceed 48 hours, beginning when a recruit arrives on campus.
Transportation	Round-trip transportation expenses may be provided by an institution or program, including actual costs for reasonable expenses incurred traveling to and from campus on the official visit. Transportation expenses may not be provided by an institution or program for parents, except for: > Transportation to campus by accompanying the recruit at the time the recruit travels in a vehicle to campus, > Transportation between campus to a bus, train station, or airport.
Parking	On-campus parking may be arranged by an institution or program.

Lodging	Lodging may be provided to a recruit and the recruit's parents or legal guardian(s) within a 30-mile radius of campus.
Meals	Meals may be provided to a recruit and the recruit's parents or legal guardian(s) up to three meals per day and a snack within a 30-mile radius of campus.
Entertainment	Entertainment may be provided to a recruit and the recruit's parents or legal guardian(s) within a 30-mile radius of campus.
Complimentary Admissions	An institution or program may provide a recruit with three complimentary admissions to a home athletics event.
Recreational Activities	Participation in recreational activities is allowed, as long as activities are neither organized nor observed by members of the athletic department. Activities may not be designed to test a recruit's abilities. Any facility used must be open to the general public.
Publicity	An institution or program may not publicize a recruit's visit to campus.

Some programs pay all of your expenses, some pay only a portion of them, and some do not cover official recruiting visit expenses at all. Coaches with limited budgets may not pay for everything for this reason. Commonly, coaches ask recruits to cover the cost of airfare, but then all lodging, meals, entertainment, and transportation to and from the airport get covered. For other official recruiting visits, the coach simply buys dinner. If you participate in an event or receive a benefit outside those listed in the table above or on the NCAA Visit Compliance Form, you may be declared ineligible by the NCAA for your collegiate athletic career.

The official recruiting visit will provide an invaluable period to develop a feel for the coaching style and team chemistry. A letter my father penned before my first official recruiting visit put the opportunity into perspective:

Dear Laura,

I am so proud of you! Official visit opportunities don't come along to every athlete or student, especially to great schools. The journey you will take over the next two months is a reflection of your hard work and perseverance. I wanted to type out some thoughts which should give you comfort going into your official recruiting visits:

1. *Swimming at any college will influence your reputation positively with colleagues and employers during school and well after graduation (i.e., many people associate athletes with being committed, disciplined, goal-oriented, competitive, etc.).*

2. *If you are undecided about your major, a college with strong programs across-the-board will be beneficial when you finally decide on what you want to focus. And remember, you can study what you're interested in, and then always go do something else for a living (i.e., college majors do not necessarily equate with particular jobs; internships can matter more than a major).*

3. *The fit of a college or university matters (i.e., if you feel happy, comfortable, and safe, you can thrive).*

4. *Just like guides on campus tours, don't let your host or the program they conduct during the visit unduly influence your impression — good or bad.*

5. *Stay engaged during your visit. Shake hands and introduce yourself to new people, make eye contact continuously, offer conversational comments, and ask lots of questions to determine your best fit (i.e., the host and people you meet should have your undivided attention).*

6. *Try to move from being a guest to being "one of them" — a part of who they are and what they are doing, as a teammate.*

7. *Be yourself and as relaxed as you can. If they get to know you, they will love you!*

Have fun with it.

Love, Dad

Here are some additional thoughts to help you get the most out of your visit, depending on what your itinerary dictates or discretionary time allows:

> **Seek out study spaces**

What is it like to study in the library? Do students study on grass fields in open spaces around campus? Do the athletes have a dedicated study area with tutors? Explore whether the academic accommodations suit your preferences for being productive.

> **Eat where the athletes eat**

On some campuses, athletes eat at a training table among themselves. On other campuses, the entire student body dines in the same location. If the latter is the case, be sure to ask how practice schedules align with dining schedules and what happens if conflicts arise.

> **Experience on-campus housing**

For one recruiting visit, coaches gave me the option of staying in a hotel or rooming with a prospective teammate on campus. Accept the latter option, if available. Spending the night in residential housing provides a great way to get to know someone and experience dorm life. It may help validate your final college selection.

> **Attend a class in a subject in which you are interested**

How big are class sizes? At large public universities, like the University of California at Berkeley, freshmen class sizes range from 450-1,500 students. At some liberal arts colleges, only eight students occupy a comfortable room. What is the teaching style? Does the professor lecture, facilitate discussion, or offer a mix of the two? How engaged are students?

> **Talk with prospective team members**

How do athletes spend time during their downtime? How do athletes balance the demands of studying, practicing, and competing? What is the culture of the team?

> **Meet with the coach one-on-one**

How best can you make contributions to the team? Where do you rank on the recruiting board? What did admissions say about your pre-read? To what extent is the admissions department aware of the recruiting visit? What degree of influence would the coach be willing to give admissions on your behalf? What are the next steps?

Here is a list of questions to consider asking during various aspects of an official recruiting visit:

When picked up at the airport by a team member

› Show enthusiasm: *It's great to be here! I'm so excited about my visit!*

› Ask about them:

  ○ Tell me about your background (e.g., hometown, hobbies)

  ○ Tell me about your role on the team (e.g., events, position)

  ○ Tell me about what you study (e.g., major, classes)

Hanging out with a host/athlete

› What are the team's goals?

› How would you describe the culture of the team?

› To what extent do athletes socialize together outside of practice?

› Do coaches expect athletes to specialize?

› Does everyone on the team travel? If not, how are those decisions made?

› Describe your experience when first joining the team.

› How, specifically, have your abilities improved since your arrival?

› What about the team has exceeded your expectations? What has not lived up to your expectations?

› How important is the sport to the school?

› How do you get assigned housing each year? Do athletes room together?

› How do you get your food each day? Do athletes eat separately or with the rest of the student body?

After attending a college class

› How similar was that class to other classes you have? How was it different?

› How available and approachable are professors?

› Are classes ever taught by teaching assistants?

Watching practice

› Is this a typical practice?

› How are practices structured?

› What is the practice schedule like during the season?

AT A PANEL ABOUT ACADEMICS

For professors:

› By when does a student have to declare a major, and is it difficult to switch majors if you change your mind?

› Do professors allow make-up work and tests missed because of practice conflicts or athletic competitions?

› How does the college support its athletes academically (e.g., tutors, study hall requirements, etc.)?

For student-athletes:

› What is a typical day like for a student-athlete on your team during the season?

› Do you find balancing academics and athletics attainable?

> How do conflicts between classes and practice get resolved?

> Are there advantages for student-athletes?

> Why did you select [College or University]?

> What is one thing you would change about [College or University]?

AT A PANEL ABOUT ADMISSIONS

> What tips do you have for completing the application? Do these vary for prospective student-athletes?

> How much does the admissions office hear from collegiate coaches about prospective student-athletes?

> Tell me about the typical profile of admitted recruits.

MEETING WITH A COACH

> Goals: What are your goals for the [gender/sport] team?

> Culture: How would you describe the culture of the team?

> Student-Athlete Balance: How are athletics and academics balanced and supported (e.g., schedules to accommodate practices, study hall, tutors if necessary)?

> Recruitment: Based on my profile, how would you envision my helping the team?

> Admissions: Tell me about the typical profile of [gender/sport] admitted recruits.

> Application Type: What expectations do you have for recruits as to how they apply (e.g., Early Decision, Early Action, Regular Decision)?

> Coaching Assistance: What leverage, if any, do you have with the admissions office for recruits?

> Process: Describe the rest of the recruiting process from here.

> Eligibility: How many credits will keep me eligible to compete? How many do I need to maintain my financial aid?

> Financial Aid: Does financial aid exist at this institution?

  ○ How much may be offered? For how many years?

  ○ What expenses besides tuition get covered (e.g., room, board, books, supplies)?

As discussed in Chapter 17, Unofficial Visits, I received the following questions during recruiting visits:

> What are you looking for in a collegiate [sport] program?

> Why do you want to come to [College or University]?

> What would you study?

> What kind of [athlete] are you?

  ○ What has your training been?

  ○ What coaching style suits you best?

> Describe a good teammate.

> What kind of teammate are you?

> What is your greatest athletic accomplishment?

> What other schools are recruiting you?

> What other schools are you considering?

On one official recruiting visit, a team boldly conducted an ice-breaker game to extract sensitive information, asking me explicit questions like: "Where are you taking official recruiting visits?" and "Which school is your top choice?"

At the conclusion of an official recruiting visit, be sure to send a thank you to the coach and your student-athlete host. Here is a sample thank you to a coach:

On Mon, Sep 19, 2016 at 12:40 AM, Laura Dickinson '17

Dear Coach,

Thank you for accommodating my recruiting visit to [College or University] this past weekend. I loved the people -- everyone from you and my host, to teammates, their friends, and other recruits. I appreciated getting your answers to my questions, swimming in [Pool Name], and simply getting a really good feel for the community. You mentioned having notes about whether I should submit test scores or not; any direction you can provide from Admissions for my application would be helpful.

I can see myself being at [College or University] and making contributions to the swimming team! While I have committed to attending each of my official visits before deciding on my preference, [College or University] has set an extremely high bar. I look forward to keeping you apprised of where I stand on recruiting over the next few weeks. Thanks again for a wonderful visit!

Sincerely,

Laura

Thank recruiting visit host(s) for sharing their weekend with you and uncovering what it means to be a student-athlete with the program at that school, like the sample below:

On Sep 25, 2016, at 11:43 AM, Laura Dickinson

Dear [Host],

Thank you for hosting my recruiting visit to [College or University] this past weekend! I really liked getting to know you better and the people at [College or University]. I particularly liked swimming in [Pool Name], playing inner-tube water polo, and going out for ice cream. I look forward to staying in touch, letting you know how my preferences take shape after recruiting visits and following your team this season. Thanks again for making me feel so welcome!

Sincerely,
Laura

Know that at the end of official recruiting visits, the coach will gather team members at a subsequent practice and ask about each prospective student-athlete on the recruiting trip. As a team, they discuss your personality, whether and how well they enjoy being with you, how interested and committed you are to their program, and anything you specifically mention that the coach should know. The most important question asked and answered is: "Would you like to have this person as a teammate?" The beginning portion of the following email illustrates this reality:

From: [Coach]
Date: September 19, 2016 at 5:09:25 PM PDT
To: "Laura Dickinson '17"
Subject: Re: Thank You!

Hi Laura,

Thanks again for coming out to visit us. I had the chance to talk with people today. You were such a huge hit with everyone - clearly you would be an amazing addition to the program. I knew that on paper so it is awesome that the team has the same feeling I do.

I talked to my liaison today to check the notes I have. Basically your strongest application will be one that includes the subject tests only. You present a very strong case and admissions recognizes it. We get the opportunity to support a handful of cases each year. I will know more about that as people make their decisions about where and when they want to apply. All I know for now is that I would be honored to be your college coach and you would make an outstanding [Team Nickname]!

I look forward to staying in touch as you narrow down your choices. Please let me know how I can help.

Have a great week!

[Coach]

If you have lingering questions about the program or where you stand, be sure to communicate with the coach:

From: [Coach]
Date: October 24, 2016 at 3:07:00 PM PDT
To: Laura Dickinson
Subject: RE: Thank You and Follow-Up Question

Dear Laura,

We enjoyed seeing you, too.

To follow-up on our conversation during your visit: We believe that you'd be an excellent academic, athletic and overall fit at [College or University] and with the [Team]. You are correct that I have a limited number of people for whom I can advocate, so I don't offer invitations lightly. If you're ready to commit to [College or University] via Early Decision, I'm ready to support your candidacy.

If you have any follow-up questions, don't hesitate to contact me. I look forward to the prospect of coaching you and please let me know when you hit "submit" on your ED application to [College or University].

Stay in touch!

[Coach]

Official recruiting visits constitute the real deal. Recruits are among the finalists for a select number of spots on a team. The coaches and team are evaluating you as much as you are evaluating them. As the number of available openings on a team and the number of recruits on an official recruiting visit suggest, expect on average a roughly 50-50 chance or worse of earning a spot on a team, varying by program and sport. Coaches often recruit four or more prospective student-athletes for every scholarship athlete signee needed. Given these odds, keeping your options open is paramount!

KEY SUMMARY POINTS:

> Official recruiting visits, often paid for by the school, involve up to 48 hours on campus with prospective coaches and teammates.

> Official recruiting visits constitute a two-way street: coaches and teammates are evaluating you as a prospective teammate, and you are evaluating your fit with the program.

> Prepare questions for each aspect of the itinerary, be prepared to answer questions from the coaches and prospective teammates, comply with NCAA guidelines about official visits, and send thank you notes after your weekend.

CHAPTER 20: **RECRUITING TACTICS BY COACHES**

Collegiate athletic recruiting is a human endeavor. Coaches face tremendous pressure to win, and now! College programs evaluate many recruits, and recruits consider many colleges. Collegiate recruiting can be a big game of chicken. Expect a two-way street. Coaches also know that many schools may be competing for the same recruit. In my case, I had rival schools at the top of their conference with campuses less than two miles apart competing for my contributions. Assistant coaches from these two rival programs even attended the same invitational meet in which I was competing over the summer between my junior year and senior year of high school. In the midst of the entire competitive process, coaches deploy some interesting, competitive, and sometimes questionable recruiting tactics.

Stories persist about the football coach that sent life-size wall posters of a prospective recruit in the college team's uniform or the basketball coach that dubbed a player into a video of one of their college games. For this chapter, I highlight tactics that I experienced that had an indirect effect on my thinking and decisions, including sending letters to parents, applying Early Decision (which is binding), holding up official recruiting visit invitations, placing time limits on accepting official recruiting invitations, offering exploding commitments, and conducting phone calls to exert pressure.

> **Sending letters to parents**

While a somewhat rare occurrence, some coaches send out letters to parents, as shown in the email provided:

From [Coach]
Date: May 14, 2016 at 9:09:30 AM PDT
To: [Laura]
Subject: Letter to your parents

Hey Laura!

I wanted to introduce myself to your parents; could you please pass this along to them?

Hello Mr. and Mrs. Dickinson,

I wanted to take a few minutes to introduce myself. My name is [Coach], and I am the Head Swimming and Diving Coach at [College or University]. I am interested in recruiting Laura for our program; but in doing this I think it is important for you to know who I am and what I believe in.

When I was in high school, I was recruited to go to a school and program who told me everything that I wanted to hear about a dream program. When I stepped onto campus, I realized that it was nothing like what I was told. The recruiters sold me a bunch of information that they knew I wanted to hear to get me there; sufficient to say that I was not happy, and I ended up dropping out after the first semester. Thinking back to this from a different perspective, I have come to realize how truly unfair this was. It was unfair to my teachers and advisors that put so much time into helping me. It was unfair to my teammates, to my friends, it was an injustice the staff did to their own team, and of course to my parents. After going through this, I took a few months to sit down and really think about what I wanted in a college experience, and what would help me feel more comfortable in the college I attended.

Now being on the other side of the process, I am committed into doing things differently. Yes, I would like to see [College or University's] Swimming and Diving Program grow, but it is not going to be through student athletes coming and leaving every year, or worse, every semester. When I talk to our recruits, like Laura, I want to help make sure that you, as a family, are making the right choice. The right choice is the one where Laura feels the most comfortable; not necessarily the easiest choice. If this is [College or University], GREAT! If not, there is a reason that there are thousands of colleges out there. There is not one place that is the perfect fit for every college bound student; and if it is not [College or University], there is bound to be a place that will be that perfect fit; and hopefully we are able to help discover what some of those qualities are as we go through the recruiting process.

For me, I like to work with our athletes, and when our first year students come in, I like to spend some good time helping them with their stroke mechanics, and help them grow and learn. In fact this is a big portion of their first year in our program. If we find students that come in, and leave after one year, this is a lot of time and effort my coaching staff and myself has put in to build a niche for Laura that goes vacant the next season. So for me it is vital that we find prospective student-athletes that are as much a good fit for us as we are for them.

With this in mind, I hope to be a resource for Laura, you, and your family as you proceed through the college search. If you have any questions about the recruiting process or about [College or University], or anything else for that matter, please feel free to contact me directly.

Thank you,
[Coach]

It's hard to tell whether this is a way to get to know a recruit's family and background, or a way to develop an in-road to influencing the decision by a recruit.

GETTING YOU TO APPLY BINDING EARLY DECISION

There are several types of applications, depending on the college: Early Decision, Restrictive Early Action, Early Action, and Regular Decision. Within Early Decision, some colleges offer Early Decision I and Early Decision II:

> **Early Decision** means that if you get admitted to that school, you must enroll unless financial aid is insufficient. In this way, a decision is binding. You may only apply to one Early Decision school but may apply to other schools Early Action or Regular Decision. Early Decision I typically involves a November 1st deadline and Early Decision II usually involves a January 1st deadline, the same deadline as most Regular Decision applications. The same commitment applies to Early Decision I and Early Decision II.

> **Restrictive Early Action** means that if you get admitted to that school, you must enroll unless financial aid is not sufficient. Unlike Early Decision, applying Restrictive Early Action to a school prohibits you from applying Early Decision or Early Action to any other school. Few schools offer the Restrictive Early Action option (e.g., Stanford, Yale).

> **Early Action** involves a non-binding admissions decision. While you learn of a school's admissions decision early, you do not necessarily have to enroll and can decide in the spring after Regular Decision announcements are received.

› **Regular Decision** constitutes the most common application approach. Apply, see if you get admitted, and then decide among the schools that want you.

To evaluate the extent of a prospective student-athlete's commitment, some coaches expect a recruit to apply Early Decision. The case, coaches argue, is that if they are going to influence your candidacy with admissions positively, they expect some degree of commitment in return. The only way to assure coaches of your commitment to them is to sign an offer letter for Division I programs or apply binding Early Decision.

While one coach indicated that I was "his top recruit," I was not invited for an official visit. He described that if I committed to the program by applying Early Decision, he could help me with admissions, as shown in the second paragraph of the email below:

From: [Head Coach]
Date: July 20, 2016 at 10:52:34 AM PDT
To: [Laura]
Subject: Applying to [College]!

Greetings from [City]!

As some of you have noticed, the [College or University] Admissions has expanded the application options by adding Early Decision I and II! Now you can choose to apply to [College or University] in the way that works best for you! You can find out all the details of each application plan HERE.

A number of you have already informed me of your intention to apply Early Action so let me know if you'll be switching to Early Decision. Those of you who haven't decided yet, keep me updated with your plan and let me know if you have questions about which option would be best for you. I'm still gathering information on how this may affect recruiting, if at all, but I'll be sure to keep all of you planning to apply to [College or University Abbreviation] updated.

Even if you're not sure when you'll be applying to [College or University] you can still get started on your application by registering for your [College or University] account and checking out our supplemental essay questions on the Admissions website. Enjoy the rest of your summer and let me know when you plan on applying to [College or University]!

GO [School Nickname]!!!

[Head Coach]
Director of Aquatics
Head Men's & Women's Swimming & Diving Coach
[College or University]

I applied Early Action instead and received a deferral from admissions. Such is the application timing dance a prospective student-athlete plays with a prospective coach.

HOLDING UP OFFICIAL RECRUITING VISIT INVITATIONS

An extension of putting pressure on a recruit to apply binding Early Decision involves holding up official recruiting visit offers. For one Midwestern college, I made an unofficial recruiting visit, submitted my pre-read materials, and maintained the assurance from the head coach that I was "at the very top of his recruiting board." I was told that the pre-read, while not a slam dunk by any means (i.e., this institution constitutes a "reach" for every applicant), was not going to hold up an invitation, according to him. After time passed following the pre-read, I inquired about the potential of an official recruiting visit. The coach indicated that he would be extending official visit invitations sometime later, even though I knew of other prospective student-athletes that had already been extended official visit invitations to the same school. Word travels. The first section of the email illustrates how an official recruiting visit invitation can be held up:

From: [Head Coach]
Date: July 21, 2016 at 9:00:39 AM PDT
To: Laura Dickinson
Cc: [Assistant Coach]
Subject: RE: Applying to [College]!

Hi, Laura!

Yes, you remain a competitive applicant. We do hold official recruiting visits in the fall but, at this moment, we would not be able to invite you out for one. We're still waiting to hear back from some other recruits first but, since we're your top choice and you will be applying EA, there's a chance we would want to invite you out for one, either this fall or in January.

Past putting you on our priority list there is not much more we can do unless we have a verbal commitment from you. There are no guarantees we would be able to offer additional support with a commitment and, even if we can, there are no guarantees you will be admitted.

Let us know if you have any other questions and thanks for the update.

[Coach]

Based on this information, the only reason I can ascertain about his delaying an official recruiting visit invitation was to see "whether other dates may be available for the prom" — I believe he wanted to see if other recruits with stronger academic or athletic credentials would surface before extending an official recruiting visit invitation. He has that right, of course. If a coach indicates a timeframe over which recruiting steps will take place, and then an unforeseen delay occurs, take caution — you may not be as high up on his or her recruiting board as conveyed previously.

After submitting my pre-read materials at another school, the coach did not invite me for an official visit, and he discouraged me from applying:

From: [Coach]
Date: August 9, 2016 at 5:46:10 AM PDT
To: 'Laura Dickinson "17"
Subject: RE: Laura Dickinson '21 Recruiting Profile

Hi Laura,

Thank you so much for sending all your information earlier this summer and I apologize for taking so long to get back to you. I've been out of the country for the last two months and just got home this past weekend.

After going through everything, reading your poem and writing sample and reviewing your transcripts, I have no doubt that you could do the work at [College or University] and make a contribution to our program. The problem right now (as I see it) is that your ACT score is not in a range that allows me to help you in the admission process. We are usually hoping to see composite scores of 33 and above. As much as I don't agree with test scores playing such an influential role in the admission process,[...] I think it's best to put that out there as early as possible so you have a good sense for where you stand.

I would be happy to stay in touch with you throughout your

college search – especially if you plan to retest this fall. Please feel free to write back if I need to clarify anything or if you have any questions at all. I'm really sorry for dropping this news on you but we've always been transparent and straight forward with our prospects so that you can make the best decisions for your college search.

Again, write or call if you have any questions and I hope you enjoy the last few weeks of summer.

[Coach]

The coach graciously wrote in a subsequent note that he didn't want me pursuing a 50-50 chance to take away an opportunity at another competitive school.

PLACING TIME LIMITS ON ACCEPTING OFFICIAL RECRUITING INVITATIONS

After conferring an official recruiting invitation, one coach indicated in a follow-up email that he expected a response as soon as possible. Somehow if I didn't act quickly enough, the offer would presumably disappear. I felt put off by this communication. In reality, coaches want full recruiting weekends. If a recruit does not accept an official visit invitation, the coach needs time to contact additional recruits to invite. If you receive multiple official recruiting visit offers, my advice is to use some time to receive potential outstanding invitations, manage invitations in hand to avoid scheduling conflicts, but then notify coaches within a short timeframe.

OFFERING EXPLODING COMMITMENTS

One "offer" from a highly-regarded liberal arts college implied a deadline or the offer would be invalid. For one, this offer came in before I completed all my official recruiting visits. What's more, like other coaches, this is a coach that could not guarantee admission; only the admissions office could make that determination. To this day, I remain very confused about what constituted the "offer." Be very circumspect about an "offer" that does not involve signing a written contract. Ask what the offer stipulates and under whose authority. Anything short of an Athletic Tender, Award Letter, Letter of Intent, or Acceptance Letter from Admissions — and ideally all four simultaneously (see Chapter 24, Pursuing an Athletic Scholarship) — does not qualify as a true "offer." Like invitations for official recruiting visits, coaches want to fill their rosters with the best prospects they can and need to know whether they can expect you to fill a slot; otherwise, they will make the "offer" elsewhere.

In response to an exploding offer, I communicated the following: "I'm honored to receive an offer to [College or University]. I made a promise to each of the coaches from whom I accepted official recruiting visits to go through that process. Keeping my word and commitment is important to me. I would like the opportunity to complete those visits before responding to your offer to make sure that I am making the right decision. I would also like to discuss the offer with my parents. For how long does your offer stand? By when do I have to make my decision?"

CONDUCTING PHONE CALLS TO EXERT PRESSURE

Throughout two-and-a-half years of corresponding with coaches in whose programs I had an interest, I never placed a phone call to them. I provided thoughtful, informative email correspondence about academic progress, club and high school team contributions, best times, and community service. Four coaches scheduled calls with me at home on which I gladly participated to gauge my ongoing interest in their programs. It was not until official recruiting visits concluded and coaches conferred offers that the phone started jumping off the hook. One assistant coach called to simply state: "You need to accept our offer this week if you want to swim with us."

While each tactic is perfectly legal and performed without malice, I believe they were testing whether their college program stood at the top of my list, how much of a priority they were, and how many other schools I might be pursuing. Under these circumstances, honesty and good etiquette will serve you well and may provide more transparency than you might otherwise expect.

KEY SUMMARY POINTS:

› A few coaches may attempt to gain your commitment by deploying various tactics.

› Be open and honest with each coach about your recruiting options, communicate where his or her program stands, and remain disciplined with your approach to honor the process and each opportunity.

CHAPTER 21: **ETIQUETTE**

Using good etiquette and appropriate behavior throughout the recruiting process is essential as it makes an impact on you and the people with whom you communicate and interact for a number of reasons:

› **Good etiquette is a reflection on you**

You only have one chance to make a first impression. How you act counts as much, if not more, than what you say.

› **You may need the practice**

Students in high school may need practice organizing themselves, maintaining discipline, communicating appropriately with adults, and responding to challenging questions.

› **It's the same things you need to do to find a job**

Let's face it, at some point you will need to prospect for a job, contact prospective employers, and interview to seek employment. The collegiate athletic recruiting process, while not the same thing, involves some of the same elements as a job search.

› **Admissions keeps a dynamic file on you**

After your first contact with an institution as a prospective student, most admissions departments open a file on you. File creation can happen as early as middle school if that is when you make your initial contact. The institution tracks *everything* — phone calls inquiring about an academic program, written correspondence, on-campus visits and activities, and recruiting visits. The admissions department wants to track how much interest you have in the school, what your interests are, and when your interest in them began. Reports from tours, information sessions, pre-reads, and recruiting visits make their way into your file. Now you know why it's called a "dynamic" file. As one prospective student-athlete on a recruiting visit opined: "You're always on."

› **Tour guides talk to admissions representatives**

A tour guide knows if you paid attention, dressed like you care, and asked thoughtful questions on a tour. The leader of the information session is probably a member of the admissions committee, so you will want to leave that person with a great impression too.

› **Coaches talk to admissions representatives**

If you rise to the level of recruit on a coach's radar, you can bet they inform admissions. Remember, a coach-recruit relationship is what sets up the pre-read and decides whether a recruit gets an invitation for an official recruiting visit.

› **Teammates influence recruiting decisions**

On recruiting visits, you will spend more time with prospective teammates than coaches. Don't forget that coaches ask teammates, "Would you want to have this person as a member of the team?"

› **Coaches talk to one another**

Coaches see each other at competitions, conferences, symposia, and if their schools are proximal, restaurants and in the gym. They compare notes and talk about recruits. Be courteous because word gets around.

› **Coaches may change teams**

A coach at a prominent engineering school in which I was not interested contacted me about swimming for them. I politely and thoughtfully replied with an email indicating that I appreciated him reaching out but that I was not interested in the school. At the same time, I kept contact for over two years with a coach at a university in the Mid-Atlantic region in which I was interested. The coach from the Mid-Atlantic university took the coaching job at an Ivy League school, and the coach from the prominent engineering school took the coaching job at the Mid-Atlantic university. Because I had been honest and steadfast with my communications, the coach that ended up at the Ivy League school tried to recruit me there, and the coach from the engineering school tried to recruit me at the Mid-Atlantic university. Respond to every contact and be honest. It may reward you later. You never know.

› **You may see a coach at a competition, league championships, or the NCAAs**

At these events, you may run into a coach with whom you interacted during the recruiting process. Having a good relationship with him or her goes a long way to making that encounter positive and less awkward.

› **You may transfer schools**

In the off-chance that you transfer colleges during your career, it will serve you well to foster supportive relationships during your recruiting process with a group of coaches on whom you can draw for a change of schools you may consider.

As a result, it is important to follow these guidelines to exhibit and maintain proper etiquette:

› **Record every contact**

This expectation requires the most discipline. By recording every contact made or received throughout the collegiate athletic recruiting process in a contact database, you will ensure the ability to recall important information.

› **Refer to your contact database to know what's been said and sent previously**

As you compile the contact database, use it to guide correspondence. Refer to its contents before composing each email or making each call to discern what has been said or sent to a particular coach, how much interest a program maintains, and changes among the coaching staff.

› **Return emails and phone calls within 24 hours**

If a prospective coach calls or writes to you, he or she expects a timely response. For one, a prompt response demonstrates an interest in their program. For another, it shows how responsive you would be if invited to be part of their team. When one coach called, it happened to be an impossible time to talk given homework, final exams, AP tests, and standardized tests. I still called back within 24 hours to schedule a call when it worked better for me. There's no harm in conducting the conversation later; the only problem is if you do not courteously return the original call within a reasonable timeframe to schedule a call for later.

›   **For schools you are not interested in, still respond**

Some people believe that emails from schools in which you are not interested can go into your computer's recycling bin. I disagree. I responded to every contact. You never know where a coach may end up. I used a short but professional response to thank a coach for contacting me while making it clear that I was not interested:

From: Laura Dickinson
Sent: Thursday, September 01, 2016 11:12 PM
To [Head Coach]
Subject: Re: [College or University] Swimming
Recruit Weekend!

Dear Coach,

Thank you for your informative messages and serious consideration. At this time, I have decided to pursue other options for swimming in college. I wish you and your team success in the future.

Sincerely,

Laura Dickinson

Here is his reply:

From: [Head Coach]
Date: September 2, 2016 at 10:50:23 AM PDT
To: Laura Dickinson
Cc: [Assistant Coach]
Subject: RE: [College or University] Swimming Recruit Weekend!

Thanks for letting me know Laura.

If you don't mind I'd like to keep you on our list, consider us your back-up, just in case you don't find what you are looking for.

Good luck in your search!

Head Coach
Swimming and Diving
[College or University]

> **Be honest**

If a prospective coach asks a question, answer it honestly. If a coach from a program in which you are not interested keeps making contact, tell him or her that you are not interested. When you get down toward the final stages of your process, tell coaches how many schools you are visiting and which ones. Tell a coach where his or her program stands. In return, they will tell you where you rank on their recruiting board. On too many occasions to count, I found that the more honest I was with a coach, the more direct he was with me. Honesty is good for both parties.

› **Say "please" and "thank you"**

Treat other people the way you would like to be treated, only better. Prospective teammates have a say in whether you get conferred an offer. How much of an influence the coach will be on your behalf with admissions may depend on how he or she and prospective teammates feel about you.

› **Write thank you notes or emails to:**

○ **Prospective coaches** after they call, attend one of your competitions, or accommodate you on an unofficial or official recruiting visit.

○ **Tour guides** for offering insights about the institution. Comment on particular aspects you recall about their background and how that relates to your interests in the school. Chapter 16, Tours and Information Sessions, includes a sample thank you letter to a tour guide.

○ **Information session leaders** thanking them for a productive session and expressing particular aspects about the school you found helpful or interesting. A sample thank you letter to an information session leader may be found in Chapter 16, Tours and Information Sessions.

○ **Your admissions office representative** by expressing interest in the college or university. These letters should be more comprehensive and showcase your writing skills; after all, they are members of the admissions committee and will probably be among the few readers of your application. Chapter 16, Tours and Information Sessions, references a letter I sent to an admissions office representative.

○ **Club team or high school coaches** when they speak to a prospective college coach or write a recommendation on your behalf. A sample thank you letter to a club team coach may be found in Chapter 28, Communicating Results and Thanking Constituents.

○ **Counselors and reference providers** when they write a recommendation on your behalf. Chapter 28, Communicating Results and Thanking Constituents, contains a sample thank you letter to a counselor and teacher.

Good etiquette ends up being a reflection of you, your high school, and others that will come after you. With research conducted, marketing completed, and visits taken, it's time to understand the financial aid and scholarship landscape.

KEY SUMMARY POINTS:

› Every communication and action you take will influence your recruitment, let alone whether you gain admission to a college or university.

› Be courteous and send thank you notes to representatives that assist you throughout the collegiate athletic recruiting process.

SECTION V: **GETTING PAID TO PLAY**

CHAPTER 22: **FINANCIAL AID**

Over $128 billion in Federal Student Aid is available from the U.S. Department of Education to fund college for students each year.[39] Each college or university provides a link on the "Financial Aid" page of its website to a "Net Price Calculator" in which information can be entered to derive the net cost for that college or university. Scholarships, grants, loans, and work-study opportunities represent various forms of financial aid.

A prospective student must complete several applications and disseminate documents before being considered for financial aid or any scholarship from a college or university:

> **Application for Admission**

Colleges do not generate awards, including athletic scholarships, until the Office of Admissions accepts a prospective student. Some coaches may request application essays as part of a pre-read, and others will want applications sent directly to them.

> **Free Application for Federal Student Aid (FAFSA)**

The FAFSA application produced by the U.S. Department of Education determines how much a family can contribute for college and how much a school should be willing to provide in financial aid to make the cost affordable. Family finances are provided on the application using principally the prior year's tax returns, savings accounts, and investment accounts. Information gets sent to the U.S. Department of Education. FAFSA applies a "Federal methodology" to determine how much a family can afford for college, which takes income and assets into account, but excludes retirement accounts and home equity. Additional information, like whether you have any siblings in college, gets submitted as well. Every family should complete a FAFSA, whether you believe you may be eligible for financial aid or not. The FAFSA application may be downloaded at *www.fafsa.ed.gov*. Each section of the application should be completed.

Note: In order to complete a FAFSA application, you need to be cleared by the Social Security Administration to receive a FAFSA ID number. This process can take five or more business days; therefore, do not commence filling out the FAFSA application less than a week before the filing deadline — the Social Security Administration may hold up your application.

› **CSS/Financial Aid Profile**

The College Board produces the CSS/Financial Aid Profile and it can be downloaded from *Collegeboard.com*. Over 800 private colleges require this application in addition to the FAFSA in order to be eligible for financial aid disbursements. An "institutional methodology" in the CSS application incorporates retirement accounts and home equity not contained in the FAFSA. As a result, the CSS institutional methodology usually results in less financial aid than the FAFSA.

› **College or University's Financial Aid Form**

Some colleges or universities require that a prospective student complete the school's customized financial aid application, in addition to the FAFSA and CSS Profile. This document is often used by the Director of Financial Aid to provide aid in special circumstances. Be sure to check and see if the college in which you are interested requires its custom financial aid form.

> **Student Aid Report**

The Student Aid Report gets generated from the FAFSA. Upon receipt, a prospective student-athlete should distribute the Student Aid Report to coaches. The report contains the Expected Family Contribution (EFC), or what a family can be reasonably expected to pay for one year of college. The Financial Aid Office at a college or university uses the EFC to determine how much in financial aid or scholarships should be conferred.

> **Financial Aid Estimator**

Used by Division II and Division III institutions, this extension of the Student Aid Report estimates the amount of aid required for a prospective student to attend a college. Some coaches use the Financial Aid Estimator to ballpark how to allocate a limited amount of money for athletic scholarships.

Each college or university stipulates a different deadline for financial aid forms. When I applied Early Decision or Early Action to some schools, financial aid forms were due by November 1st or 15th, while others were due in January, March or April. For Regular Decision applications, most financial aid forms are due by March or April. Check each college website for applicable deadlines. Schools may run out of money to allocate, so turn in applications as early as possible.

HERE ARE SOME TIPS TO MAXIMIZE FINANCIAL AID:

› Do not assume that you will not get any financial aid.

› Be prepared to show documentation and evidence for every claim on an application.

› Secure eligibility from the NCAA; coaches do not offer financial aid until you are certified.

› Defer income.

› Maximize contributions to 401Ks, IRAs, and other retirement accounts.

› Maintain satisfactory academic progress in order to be able to renew financial aid.

› Apply for financial aid every year. Like athletic scholarships, financial aid gets provided year-to-year.

Accept desired financial aid components once they are conferred. You will have the opportunity to elect whether to accept scholarships, grants, loans, and/or work-study opportunities. Electing work-study does not obligate an athlete to a job on campus; work-study can be acted upon at a later time and even declined depending on an athlete's schedule and interest. In addition to filling out financial aid forms to be considered by colleges for aid, other scholarships and awards should also be pursued by a prospective student-athlete.

KEY SUMMARY POINTS:

> Over $128 billion in Federal Student Aid is available from the U.S. Department of Education to fund college for students each year.

> Colleges do not generate awards, including athletic scholarships, until the Office of Admissions accepts a prospective student.

> The FAFSA application produced by the U.S. Department of Education determines how much a family can contribute for college (i.e., Expected Family Contribution) and how much a school should be willing to provide in financial aid to make the cost affordable.

> Over 800 private colleges require the CSS/PROFILE application in addition to the FAFSA in order for a recruit to be eligible for financial aid disbursements.

> Some colleges require completion of their own institution's financial aid application.

> Like athletic scholarships, financial aid is year-to-year and requires an application for each year of college.

CHAPTER 23: **THE TRUTH ABOUT ATHLETIC SCHOLARSHIPS**

NCAA Division I and Division II coaches and athletic directors award over $2.7 billion in athletic scholarships annually.[40] For many prospective collegiate athletes, however, the gap between total expenses — including tuition, room, board, books, and fees — and what is affordable, becomes a significant factor in choosing the college at which he or she will compete. Full rides are reserved for top-shelf athletes and often those in revenue-generating sports (e.g., NCAA I football, NCAA I basketball). Most collegiate athletes do not receive an athletic scholarship.

The NCAA limits the number of athletic scholarships and scholarship funds allowed by sport. Scholarships indicate the number of athletes receiving money, and scholarship funds represent the total cost of college in a given year times the number of scholarships allowed. Sports fall into two categories: head-count sports that only offer full grant-in-aid or nothing, and equivalency sports, where the coach may divide up a scholarship among multiple athletes. According to Lynn O'Shaughnessy of CBS Sports, "There are only six sports where all the scholarships are full ride. These so-called head-count sports are football, men's and women's basketball…women's gymnastics, volleyball, and tennis. In these Division I sports, athletes receive a full ride or no ride.[41]

Division I schools may offer athletic scholarships, with the exception of the Ivy League schools; Division II schools may also offer scholarships; however, Division III schools may not offer athletic scholarships. As of spring 2017, the table below lists the number of scholarships allowed by the NCAA per sport in Division I and Division II:

NCAA SCHOLARSHIP LIMITS

NCAA Division I Scholarships by Sport

Head Count Sports (i.e., full grant-in-aid or nothing)

Women's Sports

Basketball (15)

Volleyball (12)

Gymnastics (12)

Tennis (8)

Men's Sports

Football (85 in I-A and 63 in I-AA)

Basketball (13)

Equivalency Sports (i.e., coach may divide the scholarships among more athletes)

Women's Sports

Archery (5)

Badminton (6)

Bowling (5)

Cross Country / Track & Field (18)

Equestrian (15)

Fencing (5)

Field Hockey (12)

Golf (6)

Lacrosse (12)

Rowing (20)

Rugby (12)

Skiing (7)

Soccer (14)

Softball (12)

Squash (12)

Swimming and Diving (14)

Synchronized Swimming (5)

Team Handball (10)

Water Polo (8)

Men's Sports

Baseball (11.7)

Cross Country / Track & Field (12.6)

Fencing (4.5)

Golf (4.5)

Gymnastics (6.3)

Lacrosse (12.6)

Rifle (3.6)

Skiing (6.3)

Soccer (9.9)

Swimming and Diving (9.9)

Volleyball (4.5)

Water Polo (4.5)

Wrestling (9.9)

NCAA Division II Scholarships by Sport

Women's Sports

Archery (9)

Badminton (10)

Basketball (10)

Cross Country / Track & Field (12.6)

Equestrian (15)

Fencing (4.5)

Field Hockey (6.3)

Golf (5.4)

Gymnastics (6)

Ice Hockey (18)

Lacrosse (9.9)

Rowing (20)

Rugby (12)

Skiing (6.3)

Soccer (9.9)

Softball (7.2)

Squash (9)

Swimming and Diving (8.1)

Synchronized Swimming (5)

Team Handball (12)

Tennis (6)

Volleyball (8)

Water Polo (8)

Men's Sports

Baseball (9)

Basketball (10)

Cross Country / Track & Field (12.6)

Fencing (4.5)

Football (36)

Golf (3.6)

Gymnastics (5.4)

Lacrosse (10.8)

Rifle (3.6)

Skiing (6.3)

Soccer (9)

Swimming and Diving (8.1)

Volleyball (4.5)

Water Polo (4.5)

Wrestling (9)

Neither the Ivy League in NCAA Division I, nor NCAA Division III colleges confer athletic scholarships.

The following table from ScholarshipStats.com itemizes athletic scholarship information by gender and by team, in several NCAA Division I sports:

2016 NCAA Division I Average Athletic Scholarships by Sport

Athletic Scholarships Men's NCAA I Teams *	Teams	Average Scholarship per Team			Scholarships awarded per team		
	Teams	Average	Low	High	Average	Low	High
Baseball	299	$ 13,220	$ 6,298	$ 25,934	26	14	30
Basketball	351	$ 38,246	$ 26,896	$ 53,075	13	11	15
Football - FBS	129	$ 36,070	$ 25,237	$ 42,443	88	82	95
Football - FCS	125	$ 20,706	$ 14,474	$ 30,505	81	72	85
Golf	301	$ 12,066	$ 4,050	$ 24,018	10	6	16
Gymnastics	15	$ 18,190	$ 12,882	$ 31,573	16	14	19
Ice Hockey	60	$ 31,756	$ 19,934	$ 35,986	22	16	25
Lacrosse	70	$ 12,303	$ 8,078	$ 17,483	36	29	43
Skiing	11	$ 20,275	$ 15,478	$ 24,636	11	10	11
Soccer	205	$ 15,008	$ 5,809	$ 31,062	21	12	30
Swimming & Diving	135	$ 16,695	$ 3,112	$ 28,651	22	12	36
Tennis	263	$ 18,379	$ 6,104	$ 42,373	9	6	13
Track & Field / Cross Country	316	$ 11,260	$ 2,957	$ 24,059	29	9	59
Wrestling	77	$ 12,551	$ 5,249	$ 33,596	23	14	31

Athletic Scholarships Women's NCAA I Teams *	Teams	Average Scholarship per Team			Scholarships awarded per team		
		Average	Low	High	Average	Low	High
Basketball	349	$ 36,758	$ 21,955	$ 53,185	14	10	16
Equestrian	19	$ 10,462	$ 5,677	$ 17,196	41	36	47
Field Hockey	78	$ 18,331	$ 10,325	$ 30,012	20	17	24
Golf	263	$ 21,866	$ 8,870	$ 39,100	8	6	10
Gymnastics	63	$ 40,172	$ 23,482	$ 63,337	14	12	16
Ice Hockey	36	$ 41,693	$ 41,208	$ 42,179	20	20	20
Lacrosse	113	$ 12,884	$ 3,394	$ 22,842	31	23	38
Rowing	87	$ 21,053	$ 11,507	$ 31,771	39	19	51
Skiing	12	$ 19,084	$ 15,337	$ 23,855	12	11	14
Soccer	332	$ 17,766	$ 6,220	$ 31,363	25	17	33
Softball	295	$ 20,715	$ 7,281	$ 47,624	19	13	24
Swimming & Diving	196	$ 18,794	$ 4,552	$ 34,850	25	8	35
Tennis	323	$ 32,630	$ 13,457	$ 58,735	8	7	10
Track & Field / Cross Country	348	$ 14,574	$ 2,938	$ 26,308	32	16	61
Volleyball	334	$ 31,138	$ 12,837	$ 63,281	13	11	16

* Data includes responding schools only, programs that do not award athletic scholarships (Ivy League, etc.) are not included in these results. Number of scholarships awarded is per team, so for 4-year schools typically only 25% or so will be available for incoming (i.e., freshmen & JC transfers) student athletes.

Source: www.scholarshipstats.com/average-per-athlete.html

In nearly every sport, athletic scholarships fail to cover annual college costs of over $40,000 for public universities and $70,000 for private institutions.

The majority of athletes pay for college with academic scholarships, grants, loans, and work-study. For those that receive an athletic scholarship, they are not for all four years; athletic scholarships are year-to-year. College coaches renew scholarships annually and will usually do so unless conduct, commitment, or academic eligibility deteriorates. At some campuses within the University of California system, athletes in equivalency sports receive up to 25% of tuition in year 1 and up to 50% of tuition in year 2. Knowing that many athletes do not fulfill coaches' expectations or eventually choose not to pursue the sport, the UC system prudently provides the majority of athletic money in the back-end of a collegiate career, after knowing whether an athlete pans out.

Because financial aid decisions reside in the Financial Aid Office in a separate part of the institution, the subject of athletic scholarships can be an uncomfortable topic for most coaches. Athletes or parents should avoid initiating conversations about finances at the beginning of the recruiting process. Allowing coaches to address the subject on their terms can avoid the look and feel of a prospective student-athlete "shopping" for the best opportunity in terms of money. Ask about finances toward the conclusion of the recruiting process once you know the coach wants you and may be able to influence your admission. Playing one college's financial aid offer against another will put you in the untenable position of negotiating for the best deal, which can turn off a coach. Be sure to know what you need as a family and have the documentation to back it up. Unless the financial aid is insufficient to allow you to enroll at the college, use good judgment in bringing up the topic with a coach. You may consider approaching the Financial Aid Office instead to explore your options.

KEY SUMMARY POINTS:

> Athletic scholarships totaling $2.7 billion are available each year at NCAA programs in Division I, with the exception of the Ivy League schools, and in all Division II schools.

> The NCAA limits the number of scholarships that may be conferred by gender by sport.

> The average athletic scholarship does not come close to covering the full cost of college.

> As a result, financial aid and other scholarships should be pursued.

CHAPTER 24: **PURSUIT OF AN ATHLETIC SCHOLARSHIP**

Whereas non-athletic forms of financial aid are not typically open to negotiation, the athletic scholarship portion of an aid package may be adjusted by a coach within limits. Several steps may be taken to understand, negotiate, and finalize an acceptable athletic scholarship among multiple parties:

1. The coach and prospective student-athlete agree on the amount of an athletic scholarship for the first year of college. As previously mentioned, athletic scholarships are only conferred year-to-year.

2. An **Athletic Tender** describes the type and amount of athletic financial aid, but not other forms of financial aid. Signed by the athlete, coach, and athletic director, this document secures the athlete's commitment to the school and prohibits him or her from competing elsewhere. It is a binding contract. The Athletic Tender is contingent upon the athlete being certified by the NCAA. The NCAA uses Athletic Tenders to track compliance by the school with the number of scholarships and total amount of scholarship money given in a sport.

3. The coach and athletic director notify the Financial Aid Office

of the athletic scholarship amount by forwarding the signed **Athletic Tender.**

4. A Financial Aid Office representative summarizes all sources of financial aid — athletic and non-athletic — into an overall package itemized in an **Award Letter** sent to the student-athlete. The Award is contingent upon the athlete attending the institution and contains two important aspects:

   a. **Accept/Decline Election**. An athlete accepts or declines each form of financial aid offered.

   b. **Statement of Educational Purpose**. An athlete confirms he or she will use the financial aid for its intended purpose, remain enrolled full-time, and accept the awards.

If the athletic scholarship or financial aid offers prevent a student-athlete from enrolling, notify the coach that financial aid is a factor in your decision. Identify what your family requires for you to attend and provide the coach with the Student Activity Report generated from the FAFSA application. Inquire as to whether and how a gap between total cost and Expected Family Contribution plus financial aid can be closed with additional support. Colleges and universities provide over $12 billion, independent of federal and state sources, in financial aid from their endowments each year. Indicate that no commitment can be made until the entire financial aid picture is documented for signature.

Signed between the athletic director and student-athlete, the **Letter of Intent** jointly binds the athlete to the college or university and the institution to the athlete for the specified amount of financial aid for one year.

Let's review. The Athletic Tender does not list all financial aid being offered — only the athletic portion. It also legally binds the student-athlete to the institution, not vice-versa. The Award Letter lists all financial aid and is usually conferred after admission but is not binding, even though bowing out from a signed Award Letter would be highly unethical. The Letter of Intent is the only document which truly binds the institution to the student-athlete for the amount of financial aid conferred for one year. As a result, why would a student-athlete sign any of these documents until he or she had a Letter of Acceptance from Admissions, Athletic Tender, Award Letter, and Letter of Intent in hand? Coaches and administrations should be encouraged to provide all of the information to a prospective student-athlete so that documents may be signed simultaneously with a shared obligation.

Whether a full or partial athletic scholarship remains under consideration, non-athletic scholarships should also be pursued by every prospective student.

KEY SUMMARY POINTS:

› The awarding of athletic scholarships follows a Byzantine process involving several documents and constituents.

› Prospective student-athletes may be asked to sign documents that do not reflect the entirety of financial aid and bind him or her to the institution, without the institution making a corresponding commitment to the athlete.

› Athletes are encouraged to compile all relevant information about admission, an athletic scholarship, and financial aid before signing with a college or university.

CHAPTER 25: **NON-ATHLETIC SCHOLARSHIP OPPORTUNITIES**

In addition to athletic scholarships, student-athletes should look into all the other kinds of scholarships that are available. Finding, applying to, and receiving non-athletic scholarships and awards follow four important steps: identifying scholarships that exist; determining the mission and criteria behind each scholarship; developing your background, interests, and goals; and identifying scholarships that represent a good match for you.

Free money exists practically everywhere. One of the best ways to find potential scholarships is to research them at school, in your local community, at the library, and online. Approach your high school's college counselor to obtain a list of potential scholarships. Be sure to ask in what year applicants are eligible and for which scholarships your profile may represent a good fit. Taking advantage of a counselor's knowledge can streamline the identification of scholarships. While scholarships in the local community may not be as large as national scholarships, competition for them will be less, and even small awards add up. Sources of community scholarships include service clubs (e.g., Rotary, Kiwanis, Lions, Elks, Knights of Columbus, Soroptimist, Junior League, Boys and Girls Clubs, American Legion, American

Red Cross), religious organizations (e.g., Baptists, Catholics, Methodists, Presbyterians, Latter-Day Saints, United Church of Christ), and workers' unions (e.g., airline pilots, school administrators, municipal employees, teachers, machinists, electricians, service employees). Local newspapers often list scholarship winners from past years, which become an additional source of information. Public libraries and the internet contain directories of regional and national scholarships for consideration. Most books and online references sort scholarships by type, including extracurricular activities (e.g., Mensa, Boy Scouts, Boys and Girls Clubs, 4-H, Junior Achievement) and business (e.g., Best Buy, Coca-Cola, Dell, Microsoft, Nordstrom, Toyota), among others. Never stop looking for potential scholarships throughout high school and college.

Given that there are more scholarships available than to which you could possibly apply, opportunities need to be selectively evaluated. Behind every scholarship is an organization giving it away. Each organization desires to fulfill its mission, and conferring a scholarship to a deserving student personifies such a mission. Your challenge is to figure out what satisfies its mission and how your background and candidacy helps to advance the mission. A scholarship's mission can typically be found in the background information or press releases about a scholarship. The scholarship application itself lists the criteria used to evaluate submissions. Taken together, the mission and criteria represent what a scholarship committee is looking to reward.

Developing your profile, including interests, lists of accomplishments, and awards will help determine how well you match a scholarship's mission and criteria and how you may be differentiated among other applicants. The athletic résumé featured in Chapter 12 represents a good starting point. Sections of a college application, including honors, awards, and extracurricular activities, can be referenced as well to complete a scholarship application.

Armed with this information, you can ascertain which scholarships represent a good match based on your credentials. Pursuing scholarships takes time and effort. When completing a scholarship application, take the same amount of time you would for a college application. Complete all aspects of the application. Showcase why you deserve to be a recipient based on the scholarship's specific mission and criteria. Review entries and essays for accuracy.

I was able to earn six scholarships and awards toward my college education, independent of athletic ability, because the Division III school at which I am enrolled cannot confer athletic scholarships. Having entered the Veterans of Foreign Wars "Voice of Democracy" essay contest, I earned scholarships at post, district, regional, and state levels for my winning essay. One essay produced four checks to help fund my college education. More importantly, I dined with veterans and heard their stories of sacrifice and courage in defending our nation's freedom. The college to which I was admitted also conferred two awards to help me cover costs in my first year.

KEY SUMMARY POINTS:

> Local, regional, and national non-athletic scholarships can be identified by consulting your high school counselor, local newspapers, public libraries, and the internet.

> Develop a profile of activities and accomplishments that showcases your background, interests, and goals, and differentiates you from other prospective scholarship applicants.

> Compare your profile against the mission and criteria of each scholarship to determine to which you should apply.

SECTION VI: **MAKING DECISIONS**

CHAPTER 26: **PRIORITIZING SCHOOLS AND PROGRAMS**

The collegiate athletic recruiting process entails a multitude of decisions: which schools to evaluate, which coaches to contact, which schools to visit, how to structure application submissions, and in which school to enroll, among others. The prioritization of schools and programs along the way helps to inform these issues. Whereas Chapter 27 discusses making a final decision, this chapter deals with prioritizing options with all of the information from research, conversations, recruiting visits, and financial aid applications.

Before you can prioritize options, a student-athlete needs to understand the options available. Until you have an offer in hand (e.g., Athletic Tender, Award Letter, Letter of Intent, Letter of Acceptance), you have nothing from that school. If this is the case, maintain other options. Do not commit to a college or university until they commit — in writing — to you. If a coach is slow to produce written documentation, ask how many recruits are being pursued and where you fall in that hierarchy. I recall asking one coach, in particular, late in the recruiting process: "Where exactly do I stand on your recruiting board?"

The first decision involves whether to apply to a school Early

Decision (ED). As discussed in Chapter 20, an Early Decision application represents a binding decision. If the school admits you, you are obligated to enroll, unless in rare circumstances financial aid remains insufficient to allow you to attend. Applicants and their parents sign a contract to this effect, so it's a serious and legally-binding decision with significant ramifications if you break the agreement. Applicants can be blackballed by other schools, and your high school may suffer repercussions. One of our counselors indicated that students from our high school are rarely considered by one Ivy League school anymore because a former student reneged on his Early Decision commitment with the university.

Whether to apply ED represents a trade-off among your passion for a school of choice, the amount of support with admissions a coach may provide, and how important having that support will be for gaining acceptance versus wanting to see whether multiple schools admit you and making your choice among acceptances. If you apply Early Decision, you maximize whatever influence a coach can wield on your behalf with the respective admissions office. Applying Early Decision can also finalize your college search process if a favorable outcome arrives in mid-December. But if you apply Early Decision and get accepted, you lose the opportunity to see where else you might be able to enroll.

If you choose not to apply Early Decision, you may lose out on any influence a coach may have to help you with admissions; and worse, you may lose a spot on the team of your choosing. Early Action and Regular Decision applicants also wait up until mid-April to decide their fate.

To inform your priorities among prospective college choices, and whether one school rises to the top of the list above all others, I constructed a spreadsheet to delineate the degree to which I considered several options.

The spreadsheet sorts colleges being considered. "Mutual Contacts," "Campus Visits," and "Unofficial Visits" measure the degree of your recruiting interest in the school. "Coaches Calls," "Meets Attended by Coach," "Pre-read," "Official Visit Invitation," and "Official Visit Date" help you gauge the extent of recruitment by a coach. After combing through this information, I concluded that at least four programs really wanted me to swim for them. While the information in this exercise may be top-of-mind, summarizing your status cuts through the fog of communications with many different programs and a lengthy recruiting process to discern facts from which to draw preliminary conclusions.

Having taken official recruiting visits, if you have a clear-cut favorite among schools and programs, then apply Early Decision (ED). Be advised that you may still want or have to apply to other schools, even if you are applying Early Decision to one of the schools. You can apply Early Decision to one school and non-binding Early Action to additional schools at the same time, as long as you apply Early Decision to only one school. Also, the deadlines for applying Regular Decision to individual schools often occur before you learn about the result from the school to which you apply Early Decision. For example, I applied to my first choice college Early Decision with a November 1st deadline; the school's policy was to let applicants know about their decision on or before December 15th. Unfortunately, eight other colleges — including four private universities offering non-binding Early Action applications with deadlines by November 1st and four public universities with Regular Decision deadlines by December 1st — required application submissions before I would hear from the school to which I applied Early Decision. So despite applying Early Decision, I still submitted nine applications! Yes, I could have waited to hear from the Early Decision school before applying anywhere else, but doing so would have meant that I missed out on applying to the eight other schools;

had I not been admitted to my first choice ED, this would have been a big problem. If you are not admitted Early Decision I, then you may still be able to apply Early Decision II to the same or another school, but not all schools offer this option.

My advice would be to develop a game plan for whether and how to submit applications, based on recruiting feedback and available application cycles. I created a spreadsheet called Applications Strategy Alternatives. (Available on our website).

I used a legend as follows that helped me visually see my results.

Legend: ED1 – Early Decision 1

REA – Restrictive Early Action

EA – Early Action

RD – Regular Decision

There are several strategies I considered:

›   Option 1 involved applying to one school Early Decision I (ED1), applying to four other colleges or universities Early Action (EA) on a non-binding basis, and applying to four public universities whose deadlines occurred before I would hear from the Early Decision I (ED1) school. Regular Decision (RD) schools would be considered after considering results from the Early Decision I and Early Action cycles.

›   Option 2 considered submitting an application to one school Restrictive Early Action (REA), which would preclude me from applying Early Decision (ED) or Early Action (EA) to any other school.

›   Option 3 meant not applying to any school Early Decision I

(ED1) or Restrictive Early Action (REA), applying to schools Early Action (EA), applying to Regular Decision (RD) schools, and waiting for all decisions to choose among acceptances.

Whatever the strategy pursued, the options and overlapping deadlines among college applications compel a prospective student-athlete to draft college application essays over the summer before senior year. One way or the other, you will have many applications to complete whether you exercise the Early Decision or Restrictive Early Action options or not.

KEY SUMMARY POINTS:

> In prioritizing schools and athletic teams, one of the first decisions involves whether and to what one school to apply Early Decision (ED) or Restrictive Early Action (REA) — binding commitments if you should get in.

> Applying ED or REA represents a trade-off among your passion for a school of choice, the amount of support with admissions a coach may provide, and how important having that support will be for gaining acceptance — versus wanting to see whether multiple schools admit you and making your choice among acceptances.

> Develop and evaluate alternative application strategies among schools, being mindful of application deadlines and notification dates.

CHAPTER 27: **MAKING A FINAL DECISION**

In reality, from where you earn an undergraduate degree probably matters for securing your first job, and then in only the rarest of cases, does it matter much beyond that. At this point, you have taken advantage of many opportunities to get into college, including accentuating a specialized talent in athletics, taking solid high school courses, prepping for standardized tests, and visiting schools. Now it's time to decide on the better college for *you*.

Attending college involves taking a personal journey and realizing your passions and potential. What you become as a person long-term reflects on the personal growth that you achieve along the way. As an athlete, you learn how to take care of yourself, train arduously, eat nutritiously, and sleep well. You learn how to be prepared and perform consistently under pressure. Challenges and failure only make you stronger. In college, if you work hard in competition and the classroom, you will enjoy an unforgettable experience. Armed with a perspective on how to succeed anywhere, you cannot make a poor decision.

One of four types of admissions decisions (e.g., Early Decision, Restrictive Early Action, Early Action, Regular Decision) now arrive via email and/or the postal service. Thick manila folders usually mean acceptance and skinny envelopes often contain deferrals or rejections. Acceptance means that the school admitted you. Congratulations! A deferral indicates that the school may include your application for further consideration, usually Regular Decision. You are not in, but avoided rejection. A rejection means you will not attend that school for the academic year to which you applied.

If you reflected and completed research as outlined in this book, and then applied to institutions that fit your expectations, the colleges that accept you already meet your academic and athletic needs. Deciding which school to attend, however, takes a little more time and thought. At this point, you have invested too much time not to land your best opportunity in collegiate athletics. While every prospective student-athlete's experience is different, here is the extent of my effort — and it reads like something from the *Twelve Days of Christmas*:

47 application essays drafted

22 campuses visited

14 college applications drafted

9 college applications submitted before Early Decision notification

6 different financial aid forms submitted before Early Decision notification

6 different recommenders solicited

5 different college application formats learned

4 official recruiting visits taken

2 unofficial recruiting visits taken

1 binding Early Decision acceptance received

You will spend four or more years in classrooms, cafeterias, residential housing, and the athletic arena at a college. Choosing a college can be stressful because you do not want to make a mistake. If you followed the intentional recruiting process outlined in this book, you wouldn't make a mistake. The options available to you will suit your interests, match your capabilities, and present reliable alternatives. While you can ask people you trust for opinions, ultimately, the decision about where to go to college is up to you. Figuring out the best opportunity for you is something only you can decide.

Following are some common pitfalls to avoid in making your decision:

COLLEGE DECISION PITFALLS

›   **Putting athletics ahead of everything**

John Wooden, the successful UCLA basketball coach, remarked, "if you start putting basketball ahead of your **academics**, you're not going to have either very long."[42] While you have committed and invested heavily to stand out in your sport, choose a college as a student-athlete, and make sure the student in that designation comes first.

›   **Following peers**

Simply doing what your friends say around a high school cafeteria table, what your teammates suggest, or what a best friend might find convenient makes little sense. At this seminal moment in your life, make the best decision for you. Good friends will maintain your relationship if they are real friends, wherever you choose to enroll.

›   **Fulfilling your parents' wishes**

I have parents with alma maters. While being a legacy may help my admissions chances at their schools, and while they may feel assured that their colleges offer a great experience, "following in their footsteps" does not confer any advantage. Forge a path that makes sense for you — whether that leads to one of their alma maters or otherwise.

› **Using rankings exclusively**

A prestigious or highly-ranked school does not make it the best opportunity for you. Selectivity does not necessarily mean high quality or the right choice.

› **Relying on programs and majors**

I have no idea what I wanted to study in college, so much so that I indicated "undecided" on every college application. For colleges and universities that require you to select a school (e.g., College of Arts and Sciences, Engineering, Business, Nursing) as part of submitting an application, I remain highly skeptical. Expect that you may change majors once, twice, or even six times during your collegiate career. For this reason, I considered schools with quality programs across-the-board instead of with a particular strength in one major or another.

I ended up with four outstanding choices based on successful official recruiting visits and commitments from coaches. After completing my final recruiting visit, I cataloged my options. Two preferences stood out based on recruiting visits. The people with whom I would be associating made the biggest difference. To assess these two final options, I developed a final list of criteria, weighted them, and assigned scores to the criteria for each school:

Weighted Evaluation of Final Options

scale
1-3

	Criteria	School D		School M	
3	Feel like you belong	6	++	9	+++
1.5	weather / climate	2.25	+ 1/2	1.5	+
1	distance to pool	3	+++	1.5	+ 1/2
3	majors	3	+	3	+
1	academic requirements	1	+	1	+
2.5	dorm sizes	5	++	7.5	+++
3	food	6	++	7.5	++ 1/2
3	diversity	9	+++	6	++
1.25	pool temperature	3.75	+++	1.875	+ 1/2
1.75	indoor / outdoor pool	3.5	++	1.75	+
3	coaches	6	++	6	++
3	teammates	6	++	7.5	++ 1/2
3	people at school	6	++	9	+++
2	level of competition	6	++	2	+
1	proximity to home	2	++	1	+
3	what if not swimming?	6	++	6	++
1.5	meal payment method	1.5	+	1.5	+
1.6	size of town	1.6	+	3.2	++
2	proximity to city	4	++	2	+
1.9	potential teammates	4.75	++ 1/2	2.85	+ 1/2
3	alcohol peer pressure	9	+++	6	++
3	campus safety	7.5	++ 1/2	6	++
2.5	new experience (coast)	3.75	+ 1/2	6.25	++ 1/2
3	teachers	6	++	6	++
1.2	swag	1.2	+	1.2	+
3	employment	9	+++	6	++
1	study abroad	1	+	1	+
1	natural disasters	1	+	1	+
1	class size	1	+	1	+

125.8   116.125
123.8

As you can see, the weighted scores between the two schools ended up being very close. While this exercise was not determinative, I still had two great options. After sleeping on it for 24 hours, I made my choice. Before leaving for high school, I donned a huge smile and told my parents where I would be applying Early Decision. A sense of relief and contentment coursed through my veins

— contentment that I took this process seriously and that my efforts produced valuable information and insights. My two-plus-year collegiate athletic recruiting journey was almost over, but I would have to wait 45 days to hear the admission committee's verdict.

Once you decide on where you will apply and how, keep track of the status of deadlines and submissions. I created a chart called Master Applications and Financial Aide Schedule which helped me keep track of which cycle I was applying in; what documents I submitted among applications, test scores, transcripts, and recommendations; the status of financial aid; and when I expected to be notified.

On December 15th, I logged onto the website of the college to which I applied Early Decision to find out the admission committee's decision. Streamers of confetti digitally produced by the college cascaded down my computer screen shrouding the letter of acceptance behind it. My recruiting odyssey was over, and a new chapter at the college of my choice with a new coach and teammates would soon begin!

KEY SUMMARY POINTS:

> Ultimately, the decision about how to apply and where to enroll as a collegiate athlete is yours.

> Develop a schedule to keep track of deadlines, submissions, and notifications for admission and financial aid applications.

CHAPTER 28: COMMUNICATING RESULTS AND THANKING CONSTITUENTS

Now that you have done extensive research, identified programs in which you have an interest, learned which programs take an interest in you, conducted unofficial and official recruiting visits, read admissions decisions, and made your choice, your work is far from done.

To finish the job and help maintain a good reputation, contact the following people:

› **School at which you are enrolling.**

  ○ **Admissions.**

  Pay the non-refundable deposit to secure your place in the upcoming class.

  ○ **Financial Aid Office.**

  Elect the financial aid you choose to take. A school typically offers some combination of scholarships, grants, loans, and work-study. In conjunction with your family, choose which aspects you would like to accept.

○ **Coach.**

Write a thank you note expressing your excitement about joining the college program and appreciation for all of the assistance you received. Here is a sample letter I sent to my new college coach:

From: Laura Dickinson
Date: December 15, 2016 at 6:33:52 PM PST
To: [Coach]
Subject: Thank You!

Dear Coach,

[College or University] accepted my Early Decision application! Getting the chance to spend time with [Assistant Coach] at [School], meet with you on campus, and participate on a recruiting visit demonstrated that [Team Abbreviation] represents the perfect balance between academics and athletics. I'm excited to pursue an outstanding liberal arts education, swim for an exceptional swim team and coaching staff, and contribute to a welcoming community.

Thank you so much for being willing to advocate on my behalf! If you should have training expectations during my upcoming high school season and club team training as I prepare for next fall, please let me know.

I wish you and the entire team an enjoyable holiday season!

Sincerely,

Laura

› **Other schools to which you applied (i.e., withdrawals):**

Even if you applied Early Decision, there might be other schools to which you applied. The Early Decision language from the National Association for College Admission Counseling stipulates in its Statement of Principles of Good Practice that:

"Early Decision (ED) is the application process in which students make a commitment to a first-choice institution where, if admitted, they definitely will enroll...[Students] may have only one Early Decision application pending at any time. Should a student who applies for financial aid not be offered an award that makes attendance possible, the student may decline the offer of admission and be released from the Early Decision commitment."[43]

Withdrawing applications from other schools, after you have been accepted and send in a non-refundable deposit, is essential. Include birthdate, Social Security Number, Common Application, Coalition Application, or assigned applicant identification number as appropriate, and address, email, and phone number in case a representative from the institution needs to contact you. Below is a sample letter I sent to withdraw applications. References indicate particular schools that used particular identifying information:

To whom it may concern,

Please be advised that I am withdrawing my freshman application to the [College] for Fall 2017 enrollment. If you should have any questions, please contact me at [home phone number]. Thank you for your consideration.

Sincerely,

Laura Pedneault Dickinson

› **Other coaches that recruited you**

Whether it's other coaches who accommodated official visits or coaches with whom you corresponded for an extended period but did not visit, sending a notification and thank you is a must:

Dear Coach,

I wanted to extend the courtesy of letting you know that I will enroll at [College or University enrolling in] and swim for [Team] next year. Thank you for your excellent information and guidance about [Coach's School] College swimming. I wish you and your team much success in the future.

Sincerely,

Laura Dickinson

› **Ongoing contacts from college coaches**

Some coaches may continue to make contact thinking they hold some outside hope at landing you, even after you've let them know – following their initial contact – that you are not interested in their program.

From: [Assistant Coach]
Date: January 24, 2017 at 10:03:41 AM PST
To: [Laura]
Subject: Where are you at?

Hi Laura,

I wanted to reach out specifically to you, to see where you are at in your college search. At this point both [Coach] and I have sent you many communications and we have not heard from you in a long time. :(

The education, team environment, and overall experience you stand to gain here at [College or University] is incredible and I want you to be a part of it.

If you are interested let me know, I would love to give you a call and get to know you better.

If you are not interested, also please let me know; so I can stop wasting your time with these messages.

I hope to hear from you soon,

[Assistant Coach]
Assistant Coach - M/W Swimming & Diving

Whatever the case, maintain the level of etiquette implored in Chapter 21 and send a courteous but brief reply again.

> **Athletic websites**

Sign-in and enter the commitment to your school. In many cases, you may add a comment.

> **Current and former coaches**

Be sure to thank the people who have been instrumental to your athletic development, including present and former club team, high school, and recreational league coaches. Here is a thank you letter I wrote and emailed to my recreational swim team coach and includes his response:

On Jan 15, 2017, at 11:18 AM, Laura Dickinson

Dear [Coach],

I wanted to let you know that I will enroll at [College or University and swim for [Team] next year. I'm excited to pursue an outstanding liberal arts education, swim for an exceptional swim team and coaching staff, and contribute to a welcoming community.

Thank you for being my first swimming coach and mentoring my development at [High School]. Many of the expectations you taught me about being a good teammate, sacrificing for the team, and respecting competitors I apply as captain at [High School]. I owe this opportunity to great people like you that helped me along the way.

Good luck with the upcoming [Team] season!

Sincerely,

Laura

From: [Recreational Swimming Coach]
Date: January 16, 2017 at 7:34:24 AM PST
To: Laura Dickinson
Subject: Re: Thank You!

Congratulations Laura! That is an incredible school. The fact that you are continuing to swim in college makes me smile. Swimming in college is going to be fun, and the kids on that team are going to be lifelong friends of yours. Have a great senior season and know I am proud of you.

Love,

[Coach]

Here is the thank you letter I sent to my club team coach who spent time speaking with the college coach at the program I ended up selecting:

Dear [Coach],

[College or University] accepted my Early Decision application. I'm excited to pursue an outstanding liberal arts education, swim for an unparalleled swim team and coaching staff, and contribute to a welcoming community.

Thank you so much for being willing to advocate for me on each of my college applications. I know you conducted a telephone conversation with [Team] Coach earlier this fall. I know that your support made a real difference!

I wish you an enjoyable holiday season.

Sincerely,

Laura

> **Recommenders (e.g., counselors, teachers)**

Showing your gratitude to the people that helped you get into college(s) is important. While an email or letter may be sufficient, I hand-wrote thank you notes to the counselors and teachers that wrote recommendations on my behalf. I also included a senior picture to show my appreciation. Following is a sample thank you letter to a counselor:

Dear [Counselor],

Thank you for shepherding my [High School] journey in such a positive direction. You have been instrumental in providing me with academic rigor in and out of the classroom, and helping me pursue opportunities to serve others. I will enroll at [College or University] and swim for [Team] next year. I'm excited to pursue an outstanding liberal arts education, swim for an unparalleled swim team and coaching staff, and contribute to a welcoming community.

A couple of people made a profound difference in my [High School] experience, and you stand at the top of that list. Thank you for writing recommendations on my behalf and, more importantly, being someone on whom I could lean for guidance.

Sincerely,

Laura

Here is a sample thank you letter to a teacher that wrote a recommendation on my behalf. It is just slightly tweaked from the one I sent to a counselor:

Dear [Teacher],

Thank you for writing letters of recommendation to colleges

on my behalf. I will enroll at [College or University] and swim for [Team] next year. I'm excited to pursue an outstanding liberal arts education, swim for an unparalleled swim team and coaching staff, and contribute to a welcoming community.

A couple of people made a profound difference in my experience, and you stand at the top of that list. Thank you for inspiring my intellectual curiosity in, and making me a better student of, history. I hope you are enjoying your retirement.

Sincerely,

Laura

Once you have taken these steps, you can release a long and well-deserved exhale.

KEY SUMMARY POINTS:

> Once you decide on a school, be sure to pay the deposit, elect financial aid options, and notify the coach.

> If you applied in an early cycle to another institution, be sure to notify that school that you accepted admission elsewhere and withdraw your application.

> Write thank you notes to your current and former coaches, high school counselor(s), recommenders, parents, and others as appropriate.

SECTION VII: **DEBUNKING THE TOP 5 MYTHS ABOUT COLLEGIATE ATHLETIC RECRUITING**

THE MYTHS

MYTH #5: "THE PHONE WILL RING."

If you are a nationally-recognized athlete desired by nearly every program in the country, then this myth might be true. According to STUDENTathleteWorld.com, however, "only the top 1% of high school athletes are truly discovered."[44] For most prospective student-athletes, sending out a profile and expressing interest in a program represent the only way collegiate coaches will learn about you. Thousands of recruits compete for coveted spots on collegiate teams every recruiting season. If you are not a household name and an elite athlete, collegiate coaches will not find you on their own; they probably do not reside in your town, read your press clippings, or know your club team or high school coach. Effective pull and push marketing strategies will help "make the phone ring."

MYTH #4: "COACHES PREFER TO CONTACT PROSPECTIVE ATHLETES."

The number of roster openings in a collegiate sport exceeds the number of highly-coveted athletes available. Furthermore, coaches do not have the budget or resources to find all recruits. Listening to word-of-mouth and mining local high schools is not sufficient to fill rosters either. Coaches need to hear from prospective student-athletes interested in their program.

MYTH #3: "RECRUITING STARTS AFTER JUNIOR YEAR OF HIGH SCHOOL."

Pre-reads, official visits, and recruiting decisions typically occur during senior year of high school. Some coaches, however, make verbal offers up to two years or more before a recruit's high school graduation. According to STUDENTathleteWorld.com, "Recruiting starts behind the scenes far earlier than imagined."[45] For most prospective student-athletes, a balance needs to be struck between having something on their academic and athletic record — including high school grades and athletic performances against decent competition — versus starting the recruiting process too late. Indeed, your grades and athletic capabilities may change throughout high school. Think of starting the collegiate recruiting process sometime between the end of freshman year and the end of sophomore year.

MYTH #2: "ATHLETIC ABILITY MATTERS MOST TO COACHES."

Collegiate coaches do not want to invest their time and money recruiting an athlete who may not be admitted into their school or may become academically ineligible after enrollment. Coaches look for prospects that will be a good fit for their school and program. On top of academic and athletic capability, coaches consider character, work ethic, and coachability. If a prospect does not introduce himself or herself to a coach by using an effective push marketing effort, the coach will not be able to evaluate and decide whether to recruit the athlete.

MYTH #1: "COACHES ARE NOT COMPLETELY HONEST WITH RECRUITS."

While coaches may be different, in my experience, each coach seemed to be honest and direct throughout my recruiting process. It reinforced my confidence in the kind of people with whom I would be interacting in college. Multiple coaches on high-profile Division I teams told me: "You're not fast enough. If your times improve, contact us again." An Ivy League coach and a Mid-Atlantic coach produced times they expected a student-athlete to have to be recruited. A New England Small College Athletic Conference (NESCAC) coach expressed: "I want you on our team, but I don't know if I can get you through admissions." Every coach with whom I interacted had a strong sense about requirements for a green light from their admissions department. One coach explained, "While I cannot grant you an official recruiting visit, feel free to drop in for an unofficial visit. Just let me know in advance." Either I was not high enough on his recruiting board, or his budget was limited, but I appreciated hearing the truth, so that I could plan accordingly. Another coach indicated: "You're at the top of my recruiting board. As soon as you commit to us by applying ED (Early Decision), I will commit to you." Not only were coaches honest and direct about expectations, they genuinely wished me well in finding my best opportunity.

*

College represents a time when you will be high on autonomy and terrified of freedom. Prospective student-athletes can find their *best* opportunity by following an intentional collegiate athletic recruiting process.

**All charts, templates, diagrams, spreadsheets I used are provided for you both filled in with my information as an example and a blank downloadable version for your use. And again, Good Luck! I wish you all the best.

REFERENCES

[1] "High School Participation Increases for 25th Consecutive Year." *Nfhs news.* National Federation of State High School Associations (NFDS). 30 Oct. 2014. Web. 15 Jan 2017. <*www.nfhs.org/articles/high-school-participation-increases-for-25th-consecutive-year*>.

[2] "Estimated probability of competing in college athletics." *NCAA Research.* National Collegiate Athletic Association. 25 Apr. 2016. Web. 2 Feb. 2017. <*www.ncaa.org/about/resources/research/estimated-probability-competing-college-athletics*>.

[3] "GOALS: Growth, Opportunities, Aspirations, and Learning of Students in College." *NCAA Research.* National Collegiate Athletic Association. n.d. Web. 23 Feb. 2017. <*www.ncaa.org/about/resources/research*>.

[4] Jacobs, Peter. "Here's The Insane Amount of Time Student-Athletes Spend on Practice." *Business Insider.* Business Insider, Inc. 27 Jan. 2015. Print.

[5] "State of College Admissions 2015." *National Association for College Admission Counseling.* 2015. Web. 6 Jan. 2017. <www.nacacnet.org/news--publications/Research/>.

[6] Pachter, Aly. "Class of 2021 Early Action Admissions Rate Reaches Record Low." *The Hoya.* Georgetown University. 19 Dec. 2016. Web. 3 Feb. 2017. *<www.thehoya. comgeorgetown-early-action-admissions-rate-reaches-record-low>.*

[7] "State of College Admissions 2015." *National Association for College Admission Counseling.* 2015. Web. 6 Jan. 2017. <www.nacacnet.org/news--publications/Research/>.

[8] College Board. "The SAT Subject Tests: Student Guide." *The College Board.* 2016. Web. 6 Jan. 2017. <collegereadiness. collegeboard.org/pdf/sat-subject-tests-student-guide.pdf>.

[9] "State of College Admissions 2015." *National Association for College Admission Counseling.* 2015. Web. 6 Jan. 2017. <www.nacacnet.org/news--publications/Research/>.

[10] "Best Colleges 2017: About the Rankings/Methodology." *U.S. News and World Report.* 12 Sept. 2016. Web. 6 Jan. 2017. *<www.usnews.com/education/best-colleges/articles/ rankings-methodologies>.*

[11] Ibid.

[12] Ibid.

[13] Ibid.

[14] Ibid.

[15] Ibid.

[16] Howard, Caroline. "Top Colleges Ranking 2016: The Full Methodology." *Forbes.* n.d. Web. 6 Jan. 2017. <www. forbes.com/sites/carolinehoward/2016/07/06/ top-colleges-ranking-2016-the-full-methodology/#177ad5655b82>.

[17] "About Niche's College Rankings." *Niche.* n.d. Web. 15 Mar. 2017. <www.niche.com/colleges/rankings/methodology/>.

[18] "Academic Regulations and Requirements – usfca.edu." *USFCA. edu.* n.d. Web. 15 Mar. 2017. *<www.usfca.edu/catalog/ graduate-school-of-management/academic-regulations>*.

[19] "How To Write A High School Application." n.d. Web. 15 Mar. 2017. <//writingonlinetopessay.us/ how-to-write-a-high-school-application-essay...>.

[20] "Admission Tracker Results." *Collegedata.com.* n.d. Web. 10 Jan. 2017. *<www.collegedata.com/cs/admissions/ admissions_tracker_results_school/>*.

[21] "Questions for Student Athletes - Fastweb." n.d. Web. 10 Jan. 2017. *<www.fastweb.com/college- search/articles/ questions-for-student-athletes>*.

[22] "Top Athletic Recruiting Sites." *Top 20.* Top20Sites.com. n.d. Web. 16 Jan. 2017. *<www.top20sites.com/ top-athletic-recruiting-sites>*.

[23] "NCAA Clearinghouse. How To Register with the NCAA..." *CollegeSportsScholarships.com.* n.d. Web. 28 Feb. 2017. *<www.collegesportsscholarships.com/ncaaclearinghouse. html>*.

[24] Ibid.

[25] Ibid.

[26] "NCAA Guidelines for Camps and Clinics." *National Collegiate Athletic Association.* July 2010. n.d. 12 Feb. 2017. <tribeathletics.test.wm.edu/policies/14-c.pdf>.

[27] Ibid.

[28] Ibid.

[29] Ibid.

[30] Ibid.

[31] "NCAA Recruiting Rules. Official Visits." *CollegeSportsScholarships.com.* n.d. Web. 24 Jan. 2017. <*www.collegesportsscholarships.com/ncaa-recruiting-rules-contact-visits.html*>.

[32] "What is an unofficial visit?" *National Collegiate Athletic Association.* NCAA.org. n.d. Web. 24 Jan 2017. <*www.ncaa.org/student-athletes/future/eligibility-center/what-unofficial-visit*>.

[33] "When can I visit a college?" *AthleticScholarships.net.* n.d. Web. 24 Jan. 2017. <*www.athleticscholarships.net/question/when-can-i-visit-a-college*>.

[34] Olson, Max. "Unofficial Look at Unofficial Visits." *ESPN.* 18 Aug. 2012. Web. 24 Jan. 2017. <*www.espn.com/college-sports/football/recruiting/notebook/_/page/unofficialvisits*>.

[35] "University of Notre Dame – nd.edu." n.d. Web. 24 Jan. 2017. <www3.nd.edu/~ncaacomp/documents/IV. J. iUnofficialVisitRegulations>.

[36] "Official and Unofficial Visits1 – Office of Compliance." n.d. Web. 24 Jan. 2017. <//compliance.louisiana.edu/sites/compliance/files/Official%20and%20Unoffic>.

[37] Olson, Max. "Unofficial Look at Unofficial Visits." *ESPN.* 18 Aug. 2012. Web. 24 Jan. 2017. <*www.espn.com/college-sports/football/recruiting/notebook/_/page/unofficialvisits*>.

[38] "Official and Unofficial Visits1 – Office of Compliance." n.d. Web. 24 Jan. 2017. <//compliance.louisiana.edu/sites/compliance/files/Official%20and%20Unoffic>.

[39] Runcie, James W. "Federal Student Aid: Annual Report FY 2015." *U.S. Department of Education.* 13 Nov. 2015. Web.

6 Jun. 2017. <www2.ed.gov/about/reports/
annual/2015report/fsa-report.pdf>.

[40] Powell, Farran. "Obtaining Athletic Scholarships at NCAA
Division I Universities." *U.S. News.* 28 Apr. 2016. Web. 6
Jun. 2017. *https://www.usnews.com/education/best-colleges/
paying-for*-college/articles/2016-04-28/
decipher-athletic-scholarships-at-ncaa-division-i-
universities>.

[41] O'Shaughnessy, Lynn. "8 things you should know about sports
scholarships." 20 Sept. 2012. Web. 3 Aug. 2017. *.*

[42] "John Wooden: Basketball's Coaching Legend." *John Wooden
– Academy of Achievement.* 1963. Web. 20 Feb. 2017.
<www.achievement.org/achiever/john-wooden/>.

[43] "Statement of Principles of Good Practice – Approved by 2016
Assembly." *National Association for College Admission
Counseling.* 1 Oct. 2016. Web. 20 Feb. 2017. *<www.
nacacnet.org/globalassets/documents/advocacy-and-ethics/
statement-of-principles-of-good-practice/spgp_10_1_2016_
final.pdf>.*

[44] "Recruiting Myths." *STUDENTathleteWorld.com.* 2017. Web. 20
Feb. 2017. *<www.studentathleteworld.com/recruiting-101/
myths/>.*

[45] Ibid.

ACKNOWLEDGEMENTS

To my parents, thank you for bringing me to practices, cheering for me at meets, providing me with the opportunity to learn from great coaches, and inculcating values that will serve me well for the rest of my life.

To my teammates, thank you for your team spirit, commitment, cooperation, encouragement, and friendship.

To my instructors and coaches — Ann Curtis, Mark Anderson, Jordan Wood, John Dahlz, Ken Demont, and Don Swartz — thank you for teaching me important lessons for life in and out of the pool.

To prospective collegiate coaches with whom I came in contact, coaches with whom I carried on email conversations for over two years, and coaches who opened their programs, minds, and hearts during recruiting visits, thank you for being honest, direct, and great ambassadors of your sport.

ABOUT LAURA

A multi-sport athlete in swimming, water polo, basketball, volleyball, and tennis, **Laura Dickinson** excels in the water and on the court. Growing up, she won 38 team and individual championships in 27 seasons among these five sports. At age 10, Laura started swimming competitively in a recreational league. As her love of swimming flourished, she thoughtfully and meticulously dropped each of the other sports. On the way to her first league championships as a high school freshman, Laura suffered whiplash when a sport-utility vehicle rear-ended the sedan in which she was riding.

Wanting to swim in college, Laura endured months of rehabilitation and rededicated herself to the sport she loves. To honor the hard work she demonstrated to overcome adversity and become an accomplished swimmer, Laura conducted an intentional collegiate athletic recruiting process. One of the reasons she documented her experience throughout high school is to help teammates, friends, and prospective student-athletes around the country achieve their dream of competing in a collegiate sport. Now Laura's mission is to help prospective student-athletes successfully navigate their recruiting journeys, receive multiple offers, and earn lucrative scholarships.

Laura is a collegiate swimmer who competed at the NCAA Swimming and Diving Championships. As a high school Academic All-American, she competed in the NCSA Junior National Championships, USA Swimming Futures Championships, and California State High School Championships. Laura won three Pacific Swimming and thirteen league championships. She served as a two-time varsity team captain, earned a Coaches' Award, and garnered four letters in swimming at St. Ignatius College Prep in San Francisco. Laura is a California Interscholastic Federation/Central Coast Section Scholastic Champion and four-time Scholar-Athlete Award winner. Having directed activities for underprivileged youths in her community, Laura is also a California Scholarship Federation Life Member and Marin County Youth Volunteer of the Year. She earned six scholarships to help pay for college.

CPSIA information can be obtained
at www.ICGtesting.com
Printed in the USA
BVHW07s0416300618
520503BV00002B/7/P

9 781641 462822